"Let the same mind be in you that was in Christ Jesus. . . ."

Philippians 2:5

I do not seek to understand that I may believe, but I believe in order to understand. For this I believe — that unless I believe, I should not understand.

Anselm, *Proslogion*

ENGAGING GOD'S WORLD

A Christian Vision of
Faith, Learning, and Living

CORNELIUS PLANTINGA JR.

William B. Eerdmans Publishing Company

Grand Rapids, Michigan

Wm. B. Eerdmans Publishing Co.
2140 Oak Industrial Drive NE, Grand Rapids, Michigan 49505
www.eerdmans.com

23 22 21 20 19   19 20 21 22 23

Library of Congress Cataloging-in-Publication Data

Plantinga, Cornelius, 1946-
Engaging God's world: a Christian vision of faith, learning, and living /
Cornelius Plantinga, Jr.
p.   cm.
Includes bibliographical references.
ISBN 978-0-8028-3981-7 (pbk.: alk. paper)
1. Reformed Church — Doctrines.   2. Calvin College.   I. Title.

BX9422.3.P58 2002
230'.42 — dc21

2001058454

The epigraph from Anselm is from his *Proslogion,* Chapter I: Exhortation of the Mind to the Contemplation of God (trans. Sidney Norton Deane [Chicago: The Open Court Publishing Co., 1926], 3).

To Charles Colson,

who kneels with those who stumble

Contents

Preface for Students

In a pamphlet of 1643, the founders of Harvard College wrote their mission statement for the new school, capping it with some straight talk about the purpose of higher education. The founders said this: "Let every Student be plainly instructed, and earnestly pressed, to consider well [that] the maine end of his life and studies is *to know God and Jesus Christ which is eternall life,* Jn. 17:3, and therefore to lay *Christ* in the bottome, as the only foundation of all sound knowledge and Learning."[1]

Harvard began life in union with Jesus Christ. Its founders were Puritans, which is to say that they were English-speaking Calvinists, and they established Harvard only a few years after they had gotten off the boat at Massachusetts Bay. They could hardly wait to build a college. As a matter of fact, they and their descendants could hardly wait to build a lot of colleges. Harvard was just the beginning. According to one historian of New England, the United States had about two hundred colleges by the time of the Civil War in the 1860s, and two-thirds of them were either founded or controlled by the theological heirs of John Calvin.[2]

---

1. "New Englands First Fruits," quoted in Perry Miller and Thomas H. Johnson, *The Puritans* (New York: American Book, 1938), 702.

2. E. Digby Baltzell, *Puritan Boston and Quaker Philadelphia* (Boston: Beacon, 1979), 248.

"Something there is about Calvinism that likes a college," writes James Bratt (with apologies to Robert Frost), and this has been so from the start.[3] In 1559 the reformer John Calvin urged his local government to establish an academy in Geneva, and then he accepted an appointment as one of its first five professors. From then till now, people of Calvinist outlook have set up colleges wherever they've settled. In fact, they have lent their minds, hearts, and money to the cause of Christian higher education so often that the name of a place like Calvin College (my own alma mater) is almost redundant.

Why such enthusiasm for Christian colleges among Calvinists? No doubt one reason is that John Calvin himself loved the life of learning. Calvin understood that God created human beings to hunt and gather truth, and that, as a matter of fact, the capacity for doing so amounts to one feature of the image of God in them (Col. 3:10). So Calvin fed on knowledge as gladly as a deer on sweet corn. He absorbed not only the teaching of Scripture and of its great interpreters, such as St. Augustine, but also whatever knowledge he could gather from such famous pagans as the Roman philosopher Seneca. And why not? The Holy Spirit authors all truth, as Calvin wrote, and we should therefore embrace it no matter where it shows up. But we will need solid instruction in Scripture and Christian wisdom in order to recognize truth and in order to disentangle it from error and fraud. Well-instructed Christians try not to offend the Holy Spirit by scorning truth in non-Christian authors over whom the Spirit has been brooding, but this does not mean that Christians can afford to read these authors uncritically.[4] After all, a person's faith, even in idols, shapes most of what a person thinks and writes, and the Christian faith is in competition with other faiths for human hearts and minds.

But John Calvin's own love of learning is only one reason for the appearance of Harvard and its descendants. Long before Harvard or

---

3. James D. Bratt, "Reformed Tradition and the Mission of Reformed Colleges" (unpublished ms., Grand Rapids, 1993), 1.

4. Calvin, *Institutes of the Christian Religion,* 2 vols., ed. John T. McNeill, trans. Ford Lewis Battles (Philadelphia: Westminster Press, 1960), 1:273-74 (2.2.15); 1:270-71 (2.2.12).

the Genevan Academy, medieval Christians established universities in Paris, Oxford, Cambridge, and elsewhere, centering their study in the liberal arts. Before and alongside the universities, Christian monks preserved and extended knowledge to such a significant degree that many historians, Christian and non-Christian alike, credit the monks with saving Western civilization.

In any case, to do what comes naturally for human beings — that is, to pursue learning — Christians have wanted colleges. And to pursue learning in the light of God's Word, they have wanted *Christian* colleges — Catholic, Calvinist, Lutheran, Wesleyan, Baptist, Mennonite, independent — each with its own approach to the integration of faith, learning, and service.

What do Christians do in their colleges? What characterizes *their* approach to higher education?

Thoughtful Christians know that if we obey the Bible's great commandment to love God with our whole mind, as well as with everything else, then we will study the splendor of God's creation in the hope of grasping part of the ingenuity and grace that form it. One way to love God is to know and love God's work. Learning is therefore a *spiritual* calling: properly done, it attaches us to God. In addition, the learned person has, so to speak, more to be Christian *with*.[5] The person who studies chemistry, for example, can enter into God's enthusiasm for the dynamic possibilities of material reality. The student who examines one of the great movements of history has moved into position to praise the goodness of God, or to lament the mystery of evil, or to explore the places where these things intertwine. Further, from persistent study of history a student may develop good judgment, a feature of wisdom that helps us lead a faithful human life in the midst of a confusing world. And, of course, chemistry and history are only two samples from the wide menu of good things to learn.

But Calvin and his followers, who wanted to "reform the church

---

5. Education "develops, disciplines, and matures our humanity" and thus enables us to make a Christian profession that is "humanly significant." Henry Zylstra, *Testament of Vision* (Grand Rapids: Eerdmans, 1958), 142.

according to the Word of God," had yet another purpose in mind when they built colleges. "Reformed" Christians, as they came to be called, have always believed that getting educated is one way to prepare for service in the kingdom of God. It's not the only way, but it's an excellent way.

Certainly, if you hope to reform a church, a government, or an academy, you will need a standard to go by, and the highest and best standard for reforming all of life, so Calvin and others believed, is the written Word of God. Educated Christians therefore need to "know their Bible" in order to lead a life that fits in with the purposes of God. But to reform a complex institution — or, as a matter of fact, to write a law, treat a patient, or perform any of a number of other human undertakings — you will need to gain wisdom from many sources in addition to Scripture. You will need to look for truth wherever it may be found.

The point of all this learning is to prepare to add one's own contribution to the supreme reformation project, which is God's restoration of all things that have been corrupted by evil. The Old Testament word for this restoration of peace, justice, and harmony is *shalom;* the New Testament phrase for it is "the coming of the kingdom." You can find the Old Testament's teaching about shalom especially in the prophets, and you can find the New Testament's teaching about the kingdom especially in the Gospels and in some passages of St. Paul's epistles. According to Scripture, God plans to accomplish this project through Jesus Christ, who started to make "all things new," and who will come again to finish what he started. In the meantime, God's Spirit inspires a worldwide body of people to join this mission of God.

So when Christians strive to make God's purposes their own, they tilt forward toward God's restoration of all things, the final coming of the kingdom. They think about it, pray for it, study and work in ways that accord with it. Thinking personally as well as globally, they want the kingdom to come in their own hearts as well as in the whole world.

Admittedly, given the depth and range of evil, such cosmic restoration sometimes looks doubtful. But in a world that can be forever changed by terrorists in hijacked airliners on a bright Tuesday morning in September, restoration also looks desperately necessary. In either case, Christians live by faith in Jesus Christ, and when their faith leans forward toward the coming of the kingdom, they call it hope. The person who pursues a college education in hope, and who then shapes his or her life accordingly for service in the kingdom — such a person has a calling that will outlast every recession. The motto of Wheaton College, one of the leaders in the Christian college movement, has it exactly right: Christian higher education is "For Christ and His Kingdom."

In the case of Calvin College, its leaders stated back in 1921 that they wanted a college in which young adults would gain an education that was Christian all the way through. College faculty and staff would knead the yeast of the gospel through everything that happened on campus, so that "all the students' intellectual, emotional, and imaginative activities" would be "permeated with the spirit and teaching of Christianity."[6]

This thoroughgoing vision of Christian higher education may be traced to John Calvin, and to others before him, but its nearer proponent for Calvin College was Abraham Kuyper (1837-1920), an extraordinary Dutch theologian, newspaper editor, and prime minister. Kuyper took a large view of the Lordship of Jesus Christ, assuming that when Scripture says God has made Jesus Christ "the head over all things" (Eph. 1:22), "all" means what it says. Thus Kuyper's most famous saying: "There is not a square inch on the whole plain of human existence over which Christ, who is Lord over all, does not proclaim: 'This is Mine!'"[7] As generations have seen, the implication is staggeringly clear: those who follow Christ must bring all the parts and passions of their lives — including education — under the Lordship of Christ.[8]

6. *Yearbook of the Theological School and Calvin College,* 1916-17, 36.

7. Kuyper, *Souvereiniteit in Eigen Kring* (Amsterdam: Kruyt, 1880), 32.

8. Charles Colson's Prison Fellowship is in almost ninety nations today because Colson, from the time of his conversion, has thought globally. Prison Fellowship is a reform movement with a kingdom vision. In *How Now Shall We Live?* (Wheaton, IL:

Christians of many kinds undertake this project in many ways. Colleges in the holiness traditions may start their educational philosophy by thinking that "a holy life means a whole life," in education as anywhere else. Colleges in Lutheran and Anabaptist traditions may center their thinking on Christ's suffering servanthood and a Christian's "strength in weakness" that flows from Christ. But no matter how a Christian college plans to integrate faith, learning, and service, it will never just conduct education-as-usual — not if it is serious about Christian higher education. It won't even do education-as-usual with Bible classes tacked on, or education-as-usual with prayers before class, or education-as-usual with a service-learning component and a ten o'clock chapel break. No, a solidly built Christian college will rise from its faith in Jesus Christ and then explore the height and depth, the length and breadth of what it *means* to build on this faith — not just for four years at college, but also for a lifetime of learning and work within the kingdom of God. In short, like the Puritans at Harvard, the sponsors of top-notch Christian higher education in the twenty-first century will "lay *Christ* in the bottome."

Of course, it's one thing to start a Christian college and another thing to keep such a college Christian. Harvard University no longer functions as a distinctly Christian college, and people on its campus don't always speak well of Puritans. The same goes for most of those other Christian colleges that had been established by the time of the American Civil War. These institutions gradually slid off their foundation. We may be sobered by such slippage, but perhaps we shouldn't be surprised. Keeping a strong Christian purpose on any campus requires enormous effort. To succeed in this undertaking, a college's trustees, faculty, administration, staff, and most of its students and constituents have to work and pray in the same direction, trying aggressively to combine the whole life of the mind with the whole life of service under the headship of Christ. What's more, they must introduce this project

---

Tyndale, 1999), a celebrated statement of an evangelical Christian worldview, Colson and Nancy Pearcey list Kuyper with Calvin, C. S. Lewis, and Francis Schaeffer as their most important mentors.

to each new class of students, helping them see its strength and beauty.

Hence this book. You are holding a monograph that Calvin College commissioned me to write when I was its Dean of the Chapel. I have edited it for a wider Christian audience, but I still write as who I am — a Christian minister in the Reformed tradition who probably quotes Calvin too often. To say the theological location from which I write is "Reformed" might seem to distinguish it from, say, Lutheran, Catholic, Holiness, or Anabaptist perspectives.[9] And, indeed, there is something characteristic about the pattern of emphases within a Reformed outlook on life and learning — including, for example, an emphasis on the immensity of creation, fall, and redemption. All has been created good, including the full range of human cultures that emerge when humans act according to God's design. But all has been corrupted by evil, including not only culture but also the natural world. So all — the whole cosmos — must be redeemed by Jesus Christ the Lord. What follows is that all of life is sacred: the whole of it stands under the blessing, judgment, and redeeming purposes of God.

When Christians talk this way they are speaking with a Reformed accent, and perhaps with an Augustinian one. (The writing of the great fifth-century North African bishop, St. Augustine, is as close as we get, after Scripture, to a universal Christian voice.) Every Christian naturally speaks the faith with his own accent, and you may be used to hearing the faith spoken in tones somewhat different from the one you will find in this book. Still, I think I can say that its main lines belong to what C. S. Lewis (with thanks to Richard Baxter) called "mere Christianity," a historic, frankly supernatural vision of the triune God, creation, and their relation. This vision derives from Scripture, centers on the person and work of Jesus Christ, and grows rich from

---

9. Churches of the Swiss reformation in the sixteenth century began to call themselves *Reformed* to distinguish themselves from Lutherans, who were thought to have begun the Reformation without finishing it. Some Reformed people still think in this way about Lutherans, but politely refrain from saying so.

the contributions of ecumenical creeds, church confessions, and the thinking of such heavyweight theologians as Augustine, Aquinas, Luther, Calvin, and Barth. In these respects, I believe you will find the presentation in the pages ahead to be not only Reformed but also catholic and evangelical.

The idea in this book is to lay out some main themes of the Christian faith and to show how Christian higher education fits inside a view of the world and of human life that is formed by these themes. Perhaps you will read this book near the beginning of your Christian higher education as an introduction to it, or near the end, as a summary of it. In any case, a coherent understanding of the big themes — creation, fall, redemption, vocation, the kingdom of God, the hope of shalom — may become a kind of frame for your education, so that (if you cannot already do so) some day you will be able not merely to recognize a Christian "world and life view," but also to articulate one.

I should add that nobody assumes you will automatically *adopt* such a view. Your college leaders naturally hope that you will find this perspective inviting and, finally, compelling. But they know that you may have come to college with another scheme for organizing your ultimate loves and loyalties and that you might leave with it unchanged. Maybe you're at a Christian college only because your parents sent you there. Maybe you will change your mind about "first things" five times in four years. In any case, no human being can change your mind for you. Only the Holy Spirit can start Pentecost. Only the Holy Spirit can blow across your bow strongly enough to turn you around for good, but your college can help you hoist your sails. It can help you to see, and invite you to ponder, a Christian vision of the world and of education that we older brothers and sisters think is big, challenging, and dynamic. More important, we think it is true. We think it arises naturally from Scripture and that it possesses great power to organize and inspire human life and learning.

As author, I have tried to write straightforwardly, wanting very much not to puzzle you unnecessarily. I'm aware that readers will come to this book from many points on the spectrum of familiarity with Christian doctrine and theology and that what seems novel to some will seem old hat to others. So I've had to make a critical decision about how best to present the central ideas. I've decided to write quite simply and to use plenty of examples. In choosing this approach I run the risk of boring some of you in order, as much as possible, to avoid mystifying the rest of you. I hope my decision is right, but I'm confident that if it isn't, somebody will let me know.

After some thought, I've also decided to refer to Christians as "we" and "us," and not as "they" and "them," even though I know that some of you are not believers in Jesus Christ, or not *yet* believers. My situation is like that of Christian believers with Jewish or Muslim dinner guests. Should table prayers on such an occasion end "in Jesus' name"? I believe so. Christians mean no inhospitality to non-Christians by praying in the only way Christians know how to pray. Similarly, when I write from inside the Christian faith I naturally write as a believer and as a representative of a confessionally Christian college, but I intend no disrespect to those of you whose faith now points elsewhere.

> *The Belgic Confession contains thirty-seven articles of classic Christian teaching, starting with God and ending with the last judgment. It was written by Guido de Brès, a Reformed preacher in the Netherlands, who wrote under deadly persecution and died a martyr.*

Three other introductory notes: First, occasionally I quote the Belgic Confession (1561), the Heidelberg Catechism (1563), or the Canons of Dort (1618-19). When I quote these documents my Reformed accent will get thicker, and I hope you will still understand what I'm saying, even if you don't agree with it. In any case, I've tried

The Heidelberg Catechism, one of the confessional jewels of the Protestant Reformation, presents 129 questions and answers of remarkably warm and practical Christian piety, including wonderful treatments of the Ten Commandments, of prayer, and of "my only comfort in life and in death." The two men usually thought to have authored the document, Zacharias Ursinus and Caspar Olevianus, were only a little older than college students at the time they wrote.

The Canons of Dort contain five "canons" or norms for doctrines disputed within the Dutch churches between Jacobus Arminius, who questioned traditional Calvinist doctrine in the disputed areas, and his opponents, who defended it. The five points of doctrine, rejected by Arminius and defended by the Canons, have been popularly remembered by the acronym TULIP, to represent the doctrines of total depravity, unconditional election, limited atonement, irresistible grace, and perseverance of the saints.

to choose passages that you won't find too alarming. Second, I refer to God with masculine pronouns and titles, not because I think God is male (I don't), but simply to follow prevailing scriptural usage. Third, in referring to human beings I alternate the use of masculine and feminine pronouns in an attempt to be inclusive without awkwardly repeating "he or she," "his or her," and so forth.

I want to thank the members of the Core Curriculum Revision Committee, Calvin College, for their help in planning this monograph, and my associate Sue Rozeboom, who drafted one section of the manuscript, researched most of it, and copyedited all of it. I'd also like to thank the President of Calvin College, Gaylen Byker, for patient, intelligent guiding of the document, and the President of the Council of Christian Colleges and Universities, Robert Andringa, for his warm support of this edition. Thanks also to the following members of the faculty and staff of Calvin College who read and commented on an earlier draft: Adel Abadeer, James Bratt, Joel Carpenter, Edward Ericson, Susan Felch, David Fuentes, Lee Hardy, John Hare, Mark Hiskes, Shirley Hoogstra, Kendra Hotz, Elizabeth Howell, Thomas McWhertor, John Netland, Jeanne Nienhuis, Shirley Roels, Quentin Schultze, Franklin Speyers, James Vanden Bosch, and John Witvliet. I'd also like to thank Rimmer DeVries and George Harinck, and my colleague at Calvin Theological Seminary, Ronald J. Feenstra, who helped me with this edition.

Finally, to the students in Professor John Witvliet's Religion and Theology 201 class at Calvin College, spring of 2000, I want to say this: You read practically the whole manuscript and gave me the benefit of your thought and candor. I have learned an enormous amount from your comments and have revised the book accordingly. I will always remember with gratitude your willingness to join your professor and me in collaborating on this project. You have reminded me how good it is to live in a Christian college community through which the Spirit of God moves, inclining young and old to learn from each other as we "see visions" and "dream dreams."

Longing and Hope

As a deer longs for flowing streams,
so my soul longs for you, O God.

Psalm 42:1

O Israel, hope in the LORD!

Psalm 130:7a

Let justice roll down like waters,
and righteousness like an everflowing stream.

Amos 5:24

"In the last days it will be, God declares,
that I will pour out my Spirit upon all flesh,
and your sons and your daughters shall prophesy,
and your young men shall see visions,
and your old men shall dream dreams."

Acts 2:17 (quoting Joel 2:28)

In his novel entitled *A Separate Peace,* John Knowles gives us a memorable character by the name of Gene Forrester. In the summer of his sixteenth year Gene found that his soul was coming to life. During a stretch of glorious New Hampshire weather he would wake up each morning with a rush of feeling so profound that it overwhelmed him:

> one summer day after another broke with a cool effulgence . . . and there was a breath of widening life in the morning air, something hard to describe — an oxygen intoxicant . . . some odor, some feeling so hopelessly promising that I would fall back in my bed on guard against it. . . . I wanted to break out crying from stabs of hopeless joy, or intolerable promise, or because those mornings were too full of beauty for me.[1]

Many people would admit that they have had experiences something like this, and that they have had them especially when they were young. I say people "admit" to their longings because they are often shy about them and don't speak of them easily. And people have these longings especially when they are young because that is normally a time before we have become jaded.

Not everybody can report times of wanting to "break out crying from stabs of hopeless joy," but many do know what it feels like to yearn. People yearn for a time gone by, perhaps when their family was still together or when their friends were still in town. Or they long for a certain season, or place, or sound. For example, certain people feel a kind of delicious sadness on what seems to be the last day of summer. In *East of Eden* John Steinbeck's narrator says of the Gabilan Mountains that he wanted "to climb into their warm foothills almost as you want to climb into the lap of a beloved mother."[2] Many people know what it's like to listen to a particular piece of music that, at a certain spot, makes them ache. Mozart and Schubert knew how to touch us

1. Knowles, *A Separate Peace* (New York: Macmillan, 1959), 45.

2. Steinbeck, *East of Eden* (New York: Viking, 1952), 3.

in this way, but so do country and western singers, whose music is full of lonesome dreams and broken hearts.

> *"I have no idea to this day what those two Italian ladies were singin' about. . . . I like to think they were singin' about something so beautiful it can't be expressed in words, and makes your heart ache because of it. I tell you those voices soared, higher and farther than anybody in a gray place dares to dream. It was like some beautiful bird flapped into our drab little cage and made these walls dissolve away . . . and for the briefest of moments, every last man at Shawshank felt free."*
>
> Ellis Boyd "Red" Redding[3]

In several of his writings the Christian author C. S. Lewis explores this phenomenon of human longing or yearning — what the Germans call *Sehnsucht* (ZANE-zoocht), a word with strong overtones of seeking and searching.[4] In thinking about *Sehnsucht,* Lewis observes that when we have it, we are seeking union with something from which we are separated. For example, we want to be reunited with a happy time or a lovely place or a good friend. We look at a green valley and want to crawl under its covers. We think of a happy home and want to dwell in its center. We keep wanting to "get back" or to "get in."

3. *The Shawshank Redemption: The Shooting Script,* screenplay and notes by Frank Darabont, introduction by Stephen King (New York: Newmarket Press, 1996), 61-62.

4. See, for example, "The Weight of Glory," in *The Weight of Glory and Other Addresses,* ed. and with an intro. by Walter Hooper (New York: Collier, 1980), 3-19, and *The Problem of Pain* (New York: Macmillan, 1962), 144-54.

What's remarkable is that these longings are unfulfillable. We cannot merge with the music we love. Nor can we climb inside nature. Nature may delight us beyond telling, as Lewis says, but she cannot open her arms to receive us.[5] The same is true of future situations in our lives. We may want a good career or a family or a particular kind of life, and these things may come to us. But if so, they will not fill all our niches because we want more than these things can give. Even if we fall deeply in love and marry another human being, we discover that our spiritual and sexual oneness isn't final. It's wonderful, but not final. It might even be as good as human oneness can be, but something in us keeps saying "not this" or "still beyond." Nor can we go back into our past and steep ourselves in its joys. For one thing, some of its joys weren't as good as we think. (It's characteristically human, said Mark Twain, to remember a lot of things that never happened.) In any case, we cannot go back. Nostalgia is a yearning for what is *over* now. Places change. People change. In fact, we ourselves change enough between September and December of our first year in

> *"It would seem that Our Lord finds our desires not too strong, but too weak. We are half-hearted creatures, fooling about with drink and sex and ambition when infinite joy is offered us, like an ignorant child who wants to go on making mud pies in a slum because he cannot imagine what is meant by the offer of a holiday at the sea. We are far too easily pleased."*
>
> C. S. Lewis[6]

5. Lewis, "Weight of Glory," 14.
6. Lewis, "Weight of Glory," 3-4.

college that initial homecomings often go somewhat differently from what we might have expected.

The truth is that nothing in this earth can finally satisfy us. Much can make us content for a time, but nothing can fill us to the brim. The reason is that our final joy lies "beyond the walls of the world," as J. R. R. Tolkien put it. Ultimate beauty comes not *from* a lover or a landscape or a home, but only *through* them.[7] These earthly things are solid goods, and we naturally relish them. But they are not our final good. They point to what is "higher up" and "further back."

Perhaps the most powerful thinker among the fathers of the Christian church, St. Augustine (354-430), spent years in search of the final target of human longing. He called it the *summum bonum,* the "supreme good." Instructed by such Scripture as Psalm 42 and deeply moved by the tumult in his own soul, St. Augustine finally reached the end of his search. After years of lust ("Grant me chastity," he had prayed, "but not yet") and of philosophical exploration, he found the one good that would not fade away, the one good that would not crumble if he leaned on it with the full weight of his love. And so, in a famous prayer at the beginning of his *Confessions,* Augustine addressed the *summum bonum* of the world: "O Lord," prayed Augustine, "you have made us for yourself, and our heart is restless until it rests in you."[8]

What Augustine knew is that human beings want God. In fact, humans want union with God: they want to get "in" God, as Jesus prays in John 17:21. Until it's suppressed, this longing for God arises in every human soul because it is part of the soul's standard equipment. We have been endowed by our Creator with a *sensus divinitatis* (a "sense of divinity"), wrote John Calvin, and everywhere in the world, even when it expresses itself as idolatry, the sense of divinity is the seed of religion.[9] God has *made* us for himself. Our sense of God runs

7. Lewis, "Weight of Glory," 7.

8. Augustine, *Confessions,* trans. and with an intro. by Henry Chadwick (New York: Oxford, 1992), 145 (8.7.17); 3 (1.1.1).

9. Calvin, *Institutes,* 1:43-44 (1.3.1).

> *"Late have I loved you, beauty so old and so new: late have I loved you. . . . You were with me, and I was not with you."*
>
> St. Augustine[10]

in us like a stream, even though we divert it toward other objects. We human beings want God even when we think that what we really want is a green valley, or a good time from our past, or a loved one. Of course we *do* want these things and persons, but we also want what lies behind them. Our "inconsolable secret," says C. S. Lewis, is that we are full of yearnings, sometimes shy and sometimes passionate, that point us beyond the things of earth to the ultimate reality of God.[11] And summer mornings on which we awaken to "stabs of joy" are clues that this is so.

As a student you may have any of a number of goals for your education. Perhaps one of them should be to expand the number of things that excite your longing. Not just any things. Not just any longing. Not what corrupts or diminishes you as a person made in God's image. I'm thinking instead of "whatever is true, . . . whatever is pure, [whatever is] worthy of praise" (Phil. 4:8). I'm thinking of the visual arts, music, drama, landscapes, poetry, and friendships that can arouse human desire for sheer goodness, and finally for the One who is its overflowing fountain.

Longing as an Ingredient of Hope

But does all this talk of longing, and of what it points to, sound a little too romantic or fantastic? Do you find such talk irrelevant to the

10. Augustine, *Confessions*, 145 (10.27.38).
11. Lewis, "Weight of Glory," 6.

daily business of studying, making friends, managing your freedom, and working to support yourself?

The answer will depend, I believe, on how much you are a person who *hopes*. This is because longing is an ingredient of hope. You can hope only for something you want, and if you *really* want it, you will long for it. It's true that some of our longings are inarticulate, but others can be stated, especially when trouble intensifies them. Innocent prisoners who appeal their conviction, cancer patients who cling to rumors of experimental cures, persons who love but whose love is not returned — such folk know what they long for, and they know it urgently. So does a child who gets shunted from one stinking welfare hotel to another. For such a child, hope is as simple as it is desperate. With every fiber of her imagination, faith, and desire, this child wants a home.

According to Lewis B. Smedes, a compelling Christian thinker, genuine hope always combines imagination, faith, and desire. Those are the main ingredients. The hopeful person *imagines* a good state of affairs — the end of racism, for example. He also *believes* that it's possible. (Nobody hopes for what he's convinced is a lost cause or a logical impossibility.) Finally, he *desires* the good state of affairs he imagines and believes in; in fact, as we've just seen, his desire may rise to the level of a passion.[12]

On August 28, 1963, Martin Luther King Jr. stood before the Lincoln Memorial in Washington, D.C., and gave one of the most celebrated speeches of the twentieth century. Recalling the Emancipation Proclamation that Lincoln had signed a century before and the heroic claim of America's Declaration of Independence that the rights of life, liberty, and the pursuit of happiness are "unalienable," King lamented that black Americans "still languish in the corners of society." They still struggle through the "dark valley of segregation." It was time for black Americans to rise from their desolation, said King, and to start striding along "the sunlit path of racial justice." Taking the

12. Smedes, *Standing on the Promises: Keeping Hope Alive for a Tomorrow We Cannot Control* (Nashville: Thomas Nelson, 1998), 11-25.

voice of biblical prophecy, Martin Luther King Jr. declared it was high time for "justice to roll down like waters, and righteousness like a mighty stream" (Amos 5:24).[13]

If you have seen a videotape of the speech you may know how electric the atmosphere was in Washington that day, and how the sense of electricity kept building right along with the speech. Dr. King longed for racial justice, for a time when his own four little children would "live in a nation where they [would] be judged not by the color of their skin, but by the content of their character." He imagined a new day in which the children of slaves and of slave owners would break bread together. In a conclusion that has become famous around the world, King looked forward in faith to a day when *all* of God's children would let freedom ring!

> When we allow freedom to ring, when we let it ring from every village and hamlet, from every state and city, we will be able to speed up that day when all of God's children . . . will be able to join hands and to sing in the words of the old Negro spiritual: Free at last, free at last; thank God Almighty, we are free at last![14]

In his speech Martin Luther King Jr. incorporated all the ingredients of hope, all the power of longing, imagination, and faith. He knew that racist politics, racist laws, and racist law enforcement were wrong. He knew that racist religion was wrong and that racist hearts were all wrong. Moreover, he had the biblical passion and prophetic eloquence to shame a whole nation into *seeing* that these things were wrong. He did it by expressing biblical hope and by publicly appealing to the righteousness of God — a move that certain secularists these days think is intolerable (though they don't usually dare to say so with reference to Martin Luther King). King appealed to the righteousness of God be-

13. Martin Luther King Jr., "I Have a Dream," in *A Testament of Hope: The Essential Writings of Martin Luther King, Jr.*, ed. James Melvin Washington (San Francisco: Harper & Row, 1986), 217-19.

14. King, "I Have a Dream," 219-20.

cause he understood it as a transcendent standard of right and wrong, one that people of all kinds ought to acknowledge as the will of their Creator. In this way, as Jean Bethke Elshtain, a leading social scientist, once observed, Martin Luther King's dream was the human dream, the universal dream. His speech would never have seized a nation if he had stood before the Lincoln Memorial and stated, "I have a preference. I have a personal preference today."[15]

The most eloquent addresses to human hope and human conscience appeal to God because God's program of peace transcends racial divisions and invites us into God's "one new humanity" (Eph. 2:15). The righteousness of God transcends local prejudice and calls us to "do justice, and to love kindness, and to walk humbly with [our] God" (Mic. 6:8). In Abraham Lincoln's Second Inaugural Address the President addressed a bloodied and divided nation, holding before its citizens the plain fact that North and South "read the same Bible, and pray to the same God; and each invokes His aid against the other." But Lincoln did not regard the religious stalemate as an occasion for giving up; he regarded it as evidence that "the Almighty has his own purposes" and that they may sometimes be discerned only amid the ruin of human causes. Slavery and war are human scourges; only "the judgments of the Lord are true and righteous altogether."[16]

We should not underestimate the difficulty of discerning and following the will of God where justice is concerned. Without the lens of Scripture to correct and enlarge our vision, we see the world with self-referential bias. We can't help it. Peering out from the two sockets of our skull, we perceive, understand, and judge the world from our own point of view. We are therefore tempted to think of ourselves as centers. Moreover, we study and live in a culture that often encourages us to think in this way and, worse, to think of ourselves as our own creators and providers. But imitators of Christ, the incarnate one, struggle to see the world through the eyes of others and to focus upon *their*

---

15. Elshtain, "Everything for Sale," *Books & Culture*, May/June 1998, 9.

16. Lincoln, "Second Inaugural Address," in *Abraham Lincoln: Speeches and Writings, 1859-1865* (New York: Literary Classics, 1989), 687.

need of justice and kindness. This struggle will often begin in the simple attempt to imagine how life must be for others, and particularly how it must be for others whose situation in life differs sharply from our own. One who hopes is one who imagines.

> "To empty ourselves of our false divinity, to deny ourselves, to give up being the center of the world in imagination, to discern that all points in the world are equally centers and that the true center is outside the world, this is to consent to the rule of . . . free choice at the center of each soul. Such consent is love. The face of this love, which is turned toward thinking persons, is the love of our neighbor."
>
> Simone Weil[17]

I know that it's natural to hope for our own well-being, given our stake in it. In fact, it's not only natural to form good hopes for one's own future; it's also very healthy. To hope for your future is to affirm the life God gave you and the range of possibilities that it generates. "Keep hope alive," says Lewis Smedes, "and hope will keep you alive."[18]

---

17. Simone Weil, *Waiting for God* (New York: HarperPerennial Library, 1992), quoted in *Ordinary Graces: Christian Teachings on the Interior Life,* ed. Lorraine Kisly with an intro. by Philip Zalieski (New York: Bell Tower, 2000), 14.

18. Smedes, "Keeping Hope Alive for a Future We Cannot Control," commencement address, Calvin College, May 23, 1998.

Hoping for Shalom

But here we must keep our heads up. It's natural and healthy to hope for ourselves, but it's provincial and unhealthy to hope *only* for ourselves. Egocentric persons curve in on themselves. With only their own interests at heart, and only their own future in view, they eventually harden themselves into a small, snail-like shell. You would definitely not want to spend a week with such a person, and maybe not even a weekend. What would you talk about?

But the person who keeps her head up so that she can look out toward the future of others — this is a person with some range to her hope. This is a person who has been enlarged by the Holy Spirit. Perhaps you recall that when the Holy Spirit filled the disciples at Pentecost (an event described in Acts 2) they began to speak in multiple languages. On the day the church found its tongue it sounded like a league of nations. This wondrous phenomenon was partly the fulfillment of a hope and partly the expression of one. It fulfilled the prophetic hope of Joel:

> "In the last days it will be, God declares,
>   that I will pour out my Spirit upon all flesh,
>   and your sons and your daughters shall prophesy,
>   and your young men shall see visions,
>   and your old men shall dream dreams." (Acts 2:17)

Visions and dreams about what? About themselves and their own careers? About their own needs and the right way to meet them?

No, nothing as narrow as that. Pentecost hope came to expression in the words of Peter, the preacher for the day. Listening to the tongues of many nations, Peter stood up and declared that *everyone* who calls on the name of the Lord will be saved. The promise of God is not just for disciples and not just for Jews. This promise, said Peter at the climax of his sermon, is "for all who are far away, *everyone* whom the Lord our God calls to him" (Acts 2:39).

Here is hope that can soar because it's got some wingspan. Here,

> *The dove descending breaks the air*
> *With flame of incandescent terror*
> *Of which the tongues declare*
> *The one discharge from sin and error.*
> *The only hope, or else despair*
>   *Lies in the choice of pyre or pyre —*
>   *To be redeemed from fire by fire.*
>
>   T. S. Eliot[19]

under the influence of the Holy Spirit, one man's hope spreads out to cover all humankind. If we hope as the prophets and apostles did, then we shall hope not only for ourselves but also for people we must struggle to understand. We shall hope for people we may never have met, such as Indonesians of Chinese descent, mercilessly persecuted by their own military, or Korean Christians haunted by memories of Japanese cruelty and struggling to quiet their anger over it. We shall trust God to bring forgiveness and peace for generations we can only imagine. To do this, we need faith in the Christ whom Peter preached at Pentecost. We need faith in the resurrected Jesus, the Savior of the nations. But we also need love. Love gets us out of our shell. It lifts our interest not only toward Christ but also toward others, so that when we begin to hope, we naturally hope for them as well as for ourselves. To summarize this way of thinking, we might say (as Paul does at the end of his great hymn in 1 Corinthians 13) that biblical hope — the real thing — must have faith on one side of it and love on the other.

Biblical hope has a wide-angle lens. It takes in whole nations and

19. T. S. Eliot, "Little Gidding," in *Four Quartets* (New York: Harcourt, Brace and Company, 1943), 37.

peoples. It brings into focus the entire created order — wolves and lambs, mountains and plains, rivers and valleys. When it is widest and longest, biblical hope looks forward toward a whole "new heaven and new earth," in which death, and mourning, and pain will have passed away (Rev. 21:1, 4), and in which the Son of God receives the treasures of nations who parade into the city of God (Rev. 21:22-26).

Hope on this grand scale is just what we find in the visions of Isaiah, Joel, and the other prophets. We often think of prophets (including modern prophets) as people who cry out against evil. And so they do. They do what Martin Luther King Jr. did. Then they go to work, organizing people to fight evil and to pursue justice. They follow through on their dream so that the Spirit of God may blow upon it and make it live. Faith without works is dead (James 2:17), and the same goes for hope. Without costly action, hope can soften into sentimentality. *With* costly action, hope may harden into reality. Martin Luther King Jr. gave his life in the struggle for justice, and a whole nation's modest gains in racial understanding have become unthinkable without him.

Prophets understand evil because they also understand good. They know how many ways the world can go wrong because they also know how many ways (higher up and further back) the world can go right. And they keep dreaming of a time when God will put things right again.

Thus, the biblical prophets dreamed of a new age in which the wilderness would bloom and the mountains would drip with wine. They dreamed of a time when people would convert weapons of war into tools for harvest, of a time when a child could romp with a lion. In this coming time God would rejoice in his creation all over again. People could work in peace and work to fruitful effect, secure in the knowledge that no one would plunder their houses and vineyards. God's servants would minister justice in the earth, and all the earth would be full of the knowledge of the Lord (Isa. 32:15; Joel 3:18; Isa. 2:4; 11:6; 65:19-22; 11:9).

This webbing together of God, humans, and all creation in justice, fulfillment, and delight is what the Hebrew prophets called *sha-*

lom. We call it "peace," but it means far more than just peace of mind or cease-fire between enemies. (As a matter of fact, the area over which two armies declare a cease-fire may be acres of smoldering ruin.) In the Bible, shalom means universal flourishing, wholeness, and delight — a rich state of affairs in which natural needs are satisfied and natural gifts fruitfully employed, all under the arch of God's love.[20] Shalom, in other words, is the way things are supposed to be.

Sad to say, we now see around us only small approximations of this great state of affairs. In fact, we have a world troubled enough that human hope — sometimes wistful, sometimes desperate — will be a growth industry for some time to come. Everybody knows there is something about human life that is out of line or out of whack. We can be happy at times, but not totally fulfilled. Even when we have happiness, we fear we'll lose it. Worse, every day brings us fresh news of old evils — of nature ravaged, of God blasphemed, of people cheated, battered, terrorized. Every day brings us news of people whose misery is almost impossible to fathom.

For centuries, philosophers, theologians, novelists, and artists have described the human predicament and then prescribed a cure, or at least a salve. They have then estimated the likelihood that the prescription will work. That is, they've offered a prognosis.[21] Hope is the reach of our hearts for the cure. It's the reach of our hearts toward what we think will fulfill us, secure us, save us — and not just us, but also the whole world. To be a Christian is to participate in this very common human enterprise of diagnosis, prescription, and prognosis, but to do so from inside a Christian view of the world, a view that has been constructed from Scripture and that centers on Jesus Christ the Savior, "the Lamb of God who takes away the sin of the world" (John 1:29). Christian hope centers on Jesus Christ, the Lord of the whole cosmos, the one "through [whom] God was pleased to reconcile to

---

20. Nicholas Wolterstorff, *Until Justice and Peace Embrace* (Grand Rapids: Eerdmans, 1983), 69-72.

21. For this scheme applied to various thinkers, see Leslie Stevenson, *Seven Theories of Human Nature,* 2nd ed. (New York: Oxford, 1987).

himself all things" (Col. 1:20). Moreover, classical Christian hope centers on Jesus Christ *alone,* rejecting his rivals as pseudo-Saviors. Christians trust "no other name under heaven" (Acts 4:12).

> *"For the sinful self is not my real self, it is not the self You have wanted for me, only the self that I have wanted for myself. And I no longer want this false self. But now, Father, I come to You in your own Son's self . . . and it is He Who presents me to You."*
>
> Thomas Merton[22]

To see Christ in context, at the center of a Christian's view of the world, we now need to look in more detail at the three "acts" or "movements" of the world's drama. Drawing upon main lines of scriptural teaching, we need to review the sequence of creation, fall, and redemption, trying to see them in their interlocking connections. We do this in order to get oriented in God's world, to understand the deep background of a Christian's calling there, and, in the end, to justify our hope.

22. Thomas Merton, *Thoughts in Solitude* (Boston: Shambhala Publications, Inc., 1958), 75.

Creation

The heavens are telling the glory of God.

Psalm 19:1a

By faith we understand that the worlds were prepared by the word of God.

Hebrews 11:3a

In the beginning when God created the heavens and the earth. . . . God saw everything that he had made, and indeed, it was very good.

Genesis 1:1, 31

In [Christ] all things in heaven and on earth were created, things visible and invisible . . . all things have been created through him and for him. He himself is before all things, and in him all things hold together.

Colossians 1:16-17

The light shines in the darkness, and the darkness did not overcome it.

John 1:5

To think biblically about creation, we have to notice something that seems strange at first. When New Testament authors want to talk about God's creation of the heavens and earth, they sometimes talk about Jesus Christ. They say that creation happened "through him" or "in him" or even "for him." I say this sounds strange because we usually think of Jesus as showing up in history only a couple of thousand years ago, which is a very long time after creation. So we find it difficult to think of him acting as the mediator of creation.

It will help to recall that in classical Christian thinking *Jesus Christ* is a name and title for the eternal Son of God, the second person of the Holy Trinity. This person has always existed with the Father and the Holy Spirit. So what Christians celebrate at Christmas is not this person's coming into existence, but rather his incarnation, his birth, his presence in human flesh and spirit. In St. Paul's great hymn of Philippians 2:5-11, we read that this one person, who preexisted "in the form of God," did not cling to his divine prerogatives but "emptied himself, taking the form of a slave." He humbled himself to death. In fact, he gave himself up to death on a cross — the excruciating kind of death the Romans invented to terrorize their enemies. But this awful event also accomplished Jesus' mission in such a way that the hymn can finish with a powerful upstroke:

> [He] became obedient to the point of death —
>   even death on a cross.
> Therefore God also highly exalted him
>   and gave him the name
>   that is above every name,
> so that at the name of Jesus
>   every knee should bend, . . .
> and every tongue should confess
>   that Jesus Christ is Lord,
>   to the glory of God the Father.   (Phil. 2:8-11)

The mission of Jesus — what the Swiss theologian Karl Barth called "the way of the Son of God into the far country" — was to empty himself for the sake of others. In the mystery of the cross, the humiliating death of Jesus Christ was actually a triumph of self-giving love, an "atoning sacrifice . . . for the sins of the whole world" (1 John 2:2). That's why it brings glory to God. The point is that God's splendor becomes clearer whenever God or the Son of God powerfully spends himself in order to cause others to flourish. According to the kingdom's way of life, self-expenditure of this kind is true Lordship. And so, when the apostle Paul wants to persuade the Corinthians to join this life by making generous contributions to the poor, he refers to the pattern of the Lord:

> You know the generous act of our Lord Jesus Christ, that though he was rich, yet for your sakes he became poor, so that by his poverty you might become rich. (2 Cor. 8:9)

According to Paul, Hebrews, and the Gospel of John, Jesus Christ's pattern of life in the world reproduces the inner life of God. In John's Gospel, for example, the Father loves the Son, and the Son loves the Father back. The Father glorifies the Son, and the Son glorifies the Father back. The Son just does what he sees his Father doing. He "exegetes" God the Father because he is "close to the Father's heart." And when the Father and the Son send the Holy Spirit upon people, this "Advocate" or "Paraclete" reproduces heavenly life among these people (John 1:18; 14:26; 15:26).

At the center of the universe, self-giving love is the dynamic currency of the trinitarian life of God. The persons within God exalt each other, commune with each other, defer to one another. Each person, so to speak, makes room for the other two. I know it sounds a little strange, but we might almost say that the persons within God show each other divine *hospitality*. After all, John's Gospel tells us that the Father is "in" the Son and that the Son is "in" the Father (17:21), and that each loves and glorifies the other. The fathers of the Greek church called this interchange the mystery of *perichoresis (perry-co-RAA-sis),* and added in the Holy Spirit — the Spirit of both the Father and the Son. When early Greek Christians spoke of *perichoresis* in God, they meant that each divine person harbors the others at the center of his being. In a constant movement of overture and acceptance, each person envelops and encircles the others.

Supposing that hospitality means to make room for others and then to help them flourish in the room you have made, I think we could say that hospitality thrives within the triune life of God and then spreads wonderfully to the creatures of God. The one who spreads it is a mediator, a person who "works in the middle." We ordinarily think of Jesus Christ as the mediator of salvation, but I think we can see now that those mysterious places in the New Testament that speak of creation happening "through Christ" reveal that the agent of redemption is also the agent of creation. Christ is the person designated to work in the middle both times.

The Scriptures do not explain how Christ mediates at creation, or exactly why, but they do give us hints. They say, for example, that Christ is not only the Son of God but also the "wisdom of God" and

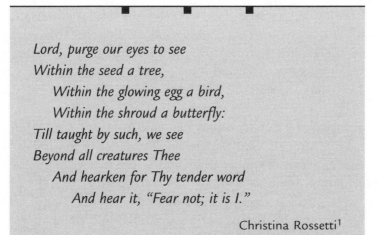

Lord, purge our eyes to see
Within the seed a tree,
   Within the glowing egg a bird,
   Within the shroud a butterfly:
Till taught by such, we see
Beyond all creatures Thee
   And hearken for Thy tender word
   And hear it, "Fear not; it is I."

Christina Rossetti[1]

1. Christina Rossetti, "Lord, purge our eyes to see," in *The Complete Poems of Christina Rossetti*, vol. 2, ed. R. W. Crump (Baton Rouge: Louisiana State University Press, 1986), 210.

the "word of God" (1 Cor. 1:24; John 1:1). These metaphors suggest that the work of Jesus Christ represents the intelligence and expressiveness of the triune God. According to God's intelligence, the way to thrive is to help others to thrive; the way to flourish is to cause others to flourish; the way to fulfill yourself is to spend yourself. Jesus himself tried to get this lesson across to his disciples by washing their feet, hoping to ignite a little of the trinitarian life in them. The idea is that if — in a band of disciples, in a family, in a college — people encourage each other, pour out interest and goodwill upon each other, favor each other with blessings customized to fit the other person's need, what transpires is a lovely burst of shalom.

The Book of Creation

"In the beginning, God created the heavens and the earth."

Creation was a way for God to spend himself. I think we are safe in assuming that God wasn't bored. God wasn't necessarily a venture capitalist, looking for a risky investment such as the human race. We may assume as well that God wasn't lonely. Nobody said, "It is not good for God to be alone. So let there be birch trees and bullfrogs and advertising executives." It's true that God cannot be God without relationships, but it doesn't follow that God needs a world in order to have them. After all, God has the endless dance of *perichoresis*,[2] the ceaseless exchange of vitality, the infinite expense of spirit upon spirit in superlative, triplicate consciousness. To speak plainly, from eternity God has had a communal life and didn't need to create a world to get one. Nothing internal or external to God compelled him to create.

But if creation is not necessary for God, neither is it an accident or a whim — as if God were doodling one day with a cosmic magic marker, drawing stick men and stick women to idle away a few thousand years of eternity, and then sighed enormously and discovered to

2. *Perichoresis* and "choreography" may share a common Greek root.

22

his amazement that the figures were starting to swell and stir with the breath of life!

Creation is neither a necessity nor an accident. Instead, given God's interior life that overflows with regard for others, we might say creation is an act that was *fitting* for God. It was so much *like* God to create, to imagine possible worlds and then to actualize one of them. Creation is an act of imaginative love. In fact, as the British author G. K. Chesterton once wrote, "the whole difference between construction and creation is . . . that a thing constructed can only be loved after it is constructed; but a thing created is loved before it exists."[3]

In creation God graciously made room in the universe for other kinds of beings. And then, out of his limitless and self-sustaining resources, God began to work. Expending vast resources of ingenuity, power, and love, God expanded the realm of being, generating ten to one hundred billion galaxies, each galaxy a stupendous bonfire of as many as one hundred billion stars, and many of the stars loaded with their own orbital systems. Over some suitable length of time, God generated great galactic wealth, and he is still generating it inside certain nebulae that are, in effect, nurseries for young stars. On our own planet, God devised processes of his own imagination to make salamanders and sandhill cranes and fringed gentians. As zoologists and botanists show us (often with a kind of wonder if they are good scientists), God's creation, as we now observe it, includes more than 750,000 species of insects and 250,000 species of plants. It includes grasshoppers that look like leaves and beetles that hitchhike on the backs of bees. Perhaps revealing a whimsical side of God's nature, creation includes the duckbilled platypus, and also "gooney" birds, a member of the albatross family found around Midway Island in the South Pacific. With their great wingspan and set-back leg placement, gooneys are champion fliers, but they visit land so seldom that, when they do, they come in for some truly foolish landings.

For Christians, the study of creation is a classic opportunity to

3. Chesterton, *Appreciation and Criticisms of the Works of Charles Dickens* (Port Washington, NY: Kennikat, 1966), 14.

read Scripture and the natural world together. Scripture tells us *who* created the wonders of the world, and why. Study of these wonders tells us, at least in part, *how* God did his wonders, and when. Both Scripture and science reveal God's nature and interests. In creation we find not only unimaginable variety but also deep orders and interdependencies. For example, plants and human beings (and many animals) need each other's exhalations. You take in oxygen and breathe out carbon dioxide, the very thing needed by a tree to live and to produce a little more oxygen for your next breath. (Is it any wonder that being in the presence of budding trees and blooming azaleas makes us feel fresher than acre upon acre of asphalt and concrete?) In this way, the world has been admirably arranged.

In creation we find creatures of wondrous particularity — each of them, and all of them, a display of God's inventiveness and love. In some marvelous chapters of the book of Job (38–41) we read that God revels in his creation. God walks in the depths of the sea, cuts water channels through deserts, and leads bear cubs out of their dens. God fathers the rain and mothers the ice. He makes a pet of the mysterious Leviathan, perhaps a sea creature (41:5). When the sea bursts from the womb, God wraps it in swaddling clothes. He also *speaks* to the sea, as if it were his own "rambunctious and exuberant child."[4] "This far you may come, and no farther," says God (38:11). And nature talks back to God. Leviathan speaks to God "with soft words" (41:3). Lightning bolts say to God, "Here we are" (38:35). And at the dawn of creation, angels and stars form into an audience and then a choir as they watch God go to work. In one spine-tingling verse, the book of Job says that God laid the foundation of the earth "while the morning stars sang together and all the angels shouted for joy" (38:7).

These highly poetic chapters do not teach us zoology, but they do teach us something important. The chapters teach us that God loves creation. God celebrates creation. God even plays with his creation. Responding in kind, an unspoiled creature turns to God with praise

4. Eleonore Stump, "Faith and the Problem of Evil," in *Seeking Understanding: The Stob Lectures, 1986-1998* (Grand Rapids: Eerdmans, 2001), 519.

> *"God leads a very interesting life and is full of joy. Undoubtedly he is the most joyous being in the universe. . . . We pay a lot of money to get a tank with a few tropical fish in it . . . but God has seas full of them, which he constantly enjoys."*
>
> Dallas Willard[5]

generated by being or acting "in character," by expressing its nature as God's creature. With perhaps Psalms 19 and 148 in mind, Daniel Migliore comments that "while the stars, the trees, and the animals do not speak or sing of the glory of God in the same way that humans do, in their own way they too lift up their praises to God, and for all we know, they do this with a spontaneity and consistency far greater than our own."[6] Humpback whales, for example, sing underwater arias; when they've finished, they often breach, soaring into an explosive half-twist back-flop with their "wings" flung wide. One researcher who studies female humpbacks and their offspring reported seeing a juvenile "leap from the water a hundred times in a row."[7] Maybe singing and breaching is the language these great beasts of the deep use to talk to God, "to cajole him, plead with him, play with him, and make covenants with him."[8]

The nonhuman parts of creation have their own particularity, just as God intended. "Each mortal thing does one thing and the

5. Dallas Willard, *The Divine Conspiracy: Rediscovering Our Hidden Life in God* (San Francisco: HarperSanFrancisco, 1998), 62, 63.

6. Migliore, *Faith Seeking Understanding: An Introduction to Christian Theology* (Grand Rapids: Eerdmans, 1991), 83.

7. Douglas Chadwick, "Listening to Humpbacks," *The National Geographic,* July 1999, 121.

8. Stump, "Faith and the Problem of Evil," 522.

As kingfishers catch fire, dragonflies draw flame;
As tumbled over rim in roundy wells
Stones ring; like each tucked string tells,
*   each hung bell's*
Bow swung finds tongue to fling out broad its name;
Each mortal thing does one thing and the same:
Deals out that being indoors each one dwells;
Selves — goes itself; myself it speaks and spells,
Crying Whát I dó is me: for that I came.

Gerard Manley Hopkins[9]

same."[10] Each human self is unique, and also the human species as a whole. But the same goes for the rest of creation. Hence the distinct "kinds" of plants and animals in Genesis 1, with each species, and each individual within its species, possessing its own integrity. As Alan Lewis notes, human beings have sometimes presumed that the sequence of creation, fall, and redemption is only a human drama. In this way of thinking, nonhuman creation is merely a stage. Animals are only props. The show is about us.[11]

But the Bible reveals the arrogance of this way of thinking. According to its revelation, "the earth is the LORD's and all that is in it" (Ps. 24:1). In Genesis 9 God makes the "rainbow covenant" with Noah, but also with "every living creature." The biblical drama that starts with

9. Gerard Manley Hopkins, "As Kingfishers Catch Fire," in *Poems and Prose of Gerard Manley Hopkins,* selected and with an intro. and notes by W. H. Gardner (New York: Penguin Books, 1953, reprint 1985).

10. Hopkins, "As Kingfishers Catch Fire."

11. Lewis, *Theatre of the Gospel* (Edinburgh: Handsel Press, 1984), cited in Migliore, *Faith Seeking Understanding,* 80.

creation and ends in shalom includes, at each stage, wolves and lambs and all else that God has made, revealing that God's providence extends beyond humankind to the whole range of created kinds. In fact, we might think of the created world as a stage not for humans, but for God, who puts on his shows in forest, sky, and sea every day.

The result, as John Calvin notes, is that "wherever we cast our gaze" we can spot signs of God's glory, disclosed in "the whole workmanship of the universe." God gives off a "general" or universal revelation through creation and providence, and unless we dull our perception of it by sloth or self-interest, the vast system of the universe becomes for us "a sort of mirror in which we can contemplate God, who is otherwise invisible."[12]

> "The universe is before our eyes like a beautiful book in which all creatures, great and small, are as letters to make us ponder the invisible things of God."
>
> The Belgic Confession, Article 2

But to do an educated job of inspecting God's workmanship, says Calvin, we have to do more than look in the mirror. We have to do more than lie on our backs and look into the night sky. We also have to study Scripture, which corrects our dull vision with its "special" or particular revelation. And then we have to study astronomy. If the universe lies before our eyes "like a beautiful book," we have to open this book. According to Calvin, anybody can spot signs of God's wisdom in creation, but especially those who have studied science and the other branches of learning. Anybody can marvel at the powers of her own brain (Calvin specifically mentions the power of memory), but a neu-

12. Calvin, *Institutes,* 1:52 (1.5.1).

rologist may marvel even more because she can use a positron emission tomography scanner to watch a remembering brain do its stuff. Those who watch get almost mystical in describing what they see. They comment on the way the hundred billion neurons of the human brain are laid out "as treelike arbors that overlap in myriad ways," with the result that when a person begins to remember, say, a first kiss, the brain does a powerful piece of synthesis, pulling up raw data (what happened) from one brain section and joining it to emotional packaging (how you felt about what happened) from another section. The result is dazzling. The signaling back and forth among all these overlapping neurons in a remembering brain looks on a scanner like the "aggregate of interactive events" in a whole Amazon jungle.[13]

Creatures of the Late Sixth Day

Of all creatures, human beings themselves — in their own minds and bodies — are a microcosm in which we can spot "unfailing signs of divinity."[14] The reason we can spot them, according to Scripture, is that we human beings have been created "in the image of God." This famous phrase appears first in the account of creation in Genesis 1, clearly at its climax. The account tells us of rhythmic bursts of work in which God creates vegetation, birds, fish, and livestock "according to their kinds." Then, in describing the events of the sixth day, the account shifts into a majestic first-person plural, a cohortative. "Let us create," says God. The narrative signals us that something weighty is about to be created — something created not according to *its* kind, but almost according to *God's* kind. It's not as if God procreates as the birds and fish do. And yet at the end of the week God does create entities that are impressively like himself, a pair of persons who can live in society and who can use their gifts to cause others to flourish:

13. Gerald Edelman, quoted in Jill Niemark, "It's Magical, It's Malleable, It's a Memory," *Psychology Today,* January/February 1995, 48.
14. Calvin, *Institutes,* 1:57 (1.5.5).

Then God said, "Let us make humankind in our image, according to our likeness, and let them have dominion. . . ." So God created humankind in his image, in the image of God he created them; male and female he created them. God blessed them and said to them, "Be fruitful and multiply, and fill the earth and subdue it; and have dominion over . . . every living thing that moves upon the earth." (Gen. 1:26-28)

This is the place in the story where activist Christians take a cue to go to work. There's so much to do in the world — so much caretaking and earthkeeping, so much filling and multiplying, so much culture to create. And, in the pages to come, we'll have occasion to think of wonderful ways for human beings to fill the earth with the fruit of their creativity — wonderful ways to get busy.

But the creation story doesn't end with a work order. The first account of creation stops after a *seventh* day. God speaks six times on six days and then stops. God rests. But each of these days also has a night. And God rests then too! God doesn't talk all the time. God doesn't work all the time. In fact, Genesis doesn't even start with a word. Genesis starts with the formlessness of the earth and with the Spirit of God brooding over the face of the deep. *Then* God speaks. You might almost say that *at last* God speaks. "Let there be light," says God. According to Genesis, God broke the cosmic silence with a creative word. Since then, the alternating silence and speech and silence is the rhythm of God, as old and deep in the nature of things as creation itself.

The idea right from the start is that there is a time to speak and a time to be silent, each in turn. There is a time to work and a time to rest from work, each in turn. We forget this because we live in a wired world where computers don't need to rest. But humans do. To say so, God in Genesis 1 does a remarkable thing. He creates human beings on the sixth day and then gives them the next day off! It's time for God's sabbath, which means it's also time for a human sabbath. Exodus 31:17 says that on the seventh day God rested and was *refreshed*, as if even God needs a break from time to time.

29

Perhaps we can't read that verse literally. But we *can* hear in it a life-giving word: our work is important, but not indispensable. Our work is important, but so is rest from work. Work is very good, but so is contemplation after work is over. And so Christians across the ages have made space in their lives to honor God's sabbath — a space for worship, for refreshment, for the silence that comes from the very rhythm of God.

> *"When we have met our Lord in the silent intimacy of our prayer, then we will also meet him . . . in the market, and in the town square. But when we have not met him in the center of our own hearts, we cannot expect to meet him in the busyness of our daily lives."*
>
> Henri Nouwen[15]

I do not believe we should think of silences as inert. They may be full of thought, of meditation, of reflection on whatever is "worthy of praise" (Phil. 4:8). Good silences may fill us with longing for shalom or with listening for God. Silence lets us brood over things that make us deep. Silence may become a cradle of delight.

How are human beings like God? They are beings of speech and silence, of work and rest, each in its place, each in its turn.

How else are human beings like God? Pulling central scriptural teaching from Genesis, John, and Paul, let's count three ways.

First, God gives human beings authority in the created world, what we might call "responsible dominion." Here is the first big work project. God the king assigns sub-kingdoms in which, under God, we

15. Henri Nouwen, *¡Gracias!: A Latin American Journal* (San Francisco: Harper & Row, 1983), 21.

human beings have our say. "Let them have dominion," says God. Let them take responsibility for keeping the earth, for respecting the integrity of kinds, and times, and seasons. Let human beings discover the character of other creatures and do what they can to assist these creatures to act in character.

As you may know, a controversy has been brewing over this feature of the image of God. Critics charge Jews and Christians with turning Genesis dominion into a license for trashing the earth instead of keeping it, for exploiting animals instead of husbanding them. And, sorry to say, some of this criticism is on the mark. Christians and others have sometimes taken dominion as justification for the "conquest" of nature — language that once appeared routinely in social science textbooks.[16] The language of conquest suggested that we humans were at war with God's nonhuman creation, that roaming herds and burgeoning forests were somehow our enemy. Such language showed that we had lost the biblical portrait of shalom and that we needed to repent and recover it.

Nonetheless, the Bible is not the problem here. The Bible speaks of dominion, not in the sense of conquest, but in the sense of *stewardship*. After all, how does God himself exercise dominion? How does God demonstrate hospitality in creation and providence?

In the kingdom of God that Jesus proclaimed, dominion is never "lording over"; it's more like "lording under" by way of support. In the kingdom of God, to have dominion is to care for the well-being of others. To have dominion is to act like the mediator of creation. This means that a human steward of God's good creation will never exploit or pillage; instead, she will give creation room to be itself. She will respect it, care for it, empower it. Her goal is to live in healthy interdependence with it. The person who practices good animal husbandry, forest management, and water conservation shows respect for God by showing respect for what God has made.

But God's creation extends beyond the biophysical sphere to include a vast array of cultural possibilities that God folded into human

16. Migliore, *Faith Seeking Understanding*, 81-84.

> *Cultural Mandate: God's charge to our first parents to "transform untamed nature into a social environment" by cultural formation that fits God's design.*
>
> Richard Mouw[17]

nature. Thus, in the "cultural mandate" of Genesis 1:28, God charges humankind to be "fruitful and multiply," to *"fill the earth and subdue it."* According to a widespread interpretation of this mandate (or is it a blessing?), God's good creation includes not only earth and its creatures, but also an array of cultural gifts, such as marriage, family, art, language, commerce, and (even in an ideal world) government. The fall into sin has corrupted these gifts but hasn't unlicensed them. The same goes for the cultural initiatives we discover in Genesis 4, that is, urban development, tent-making, musicianship, and metal-working.[18] All of these unfold the built-in potential of God's creation. All reflect the ingenuity of God's human creatures — itself a superb example of likeness to God. After the building trades had been corrupted for millennia (having been used to build Babel and Babylon, for example) Jesus adopted one of them as his own. Cities themselves are God's idea. Good urban landscape management is a godly occupation. After centuries of urban crime and decay, the destination of redeemed people is not a return ticket to the garden of Eden, but entry into "the holy city, the new Jerusalem" (Rev. 21:2). Because "the earth is the LORD's and the fullness thereof" (Ps. 24:1, RSV), all the centuries of human obedience to the cultural mandate will have produced some treasure by the end — trash, too, but also treasure. If this is the "fullness" that belongs to

17. Richard J. Mouw, *When the Kings Come Marching In: Isaiah and the New Jerusalem* (Grand Rapids: Eerdmans, 1983), 16.

18. Henk Aay reminded me of this point and of its relevance here.

God, then we may think of the holy city as the garden of Eden plus the fullness of the centuries.[19]

To image God, then, human beings are charged not only with care for earth and animals ("subduing" what's already there) but also with developing certain cultural possibilities ("filling" out what is only potentially there). To unfold such possibilities — for example, to speak languages, build tools and dies, enter contracts, organize dance troupes — is to act in character for human beings designed by God. That is, to act in this way is to exhibit some of God's own creativity and dominion in a characteristically human way.

Second, we image God when we live in loving communion with each other. Because God is triune, the image of God is social as well as personal. God lives in the perichoretic glory of a three-person community, radiant with love, joy, power, and beauty. Each person is God only *with* the other two. Each of the persons is essentially divine by the same pattern of excellences, such as sovereign love and power. "The Father is God, the Son is God, and the Holy Spirit is God," as the Athanasian Creed says. And yet "there is only one God," the holy Trinity itself, a union of three mutually enveloping persons.

What's the connection to us? In chapter 17 of John's Gospel Jesus prays for the disciples and for new believers who would be brought into the disciples' community by evangelism. Thinking of his relationship with God the Father, Jesus prays that "they may be one, as we are one" (17:22). By "they" Jesus means the community of believers. Jesus' prayer reveals that when we live in strong unity and harmony with others we are something like God. Perhaps this might be true of a marriage, for example, or of an extraordinarily faithful and intimate friendship. But the one biblically authorized analogy for the Holy Trinity is the church, the "new community" that Jesus prays for and with which he compares his life with the Father.

When we turn to Paul, we find John's picture enlarged. Paul writes to churches who are squabbling and tells them to stop. He then offers them a recipe for communal love. To follow it, members

19. Mouw, *When the Kings Come Marching In,* 17.

of the church have to live peaceably, forgive one another, and work faithfully so as to be able to give to the poor. They have to hate what is evil, love what is good, practice hospitality, and be patient with whoever drives them nuts. To do these things is to be like God. To act like this is to act like God. More specifically, to accept such straightforward duties as speaking the truth to our neighbor (Eph. 4:25) is to follow Jesus, who is the preeminent image of God the Father (Col. 1:15; 2 Cor. 4:4). We image God by imaging Christ, and we do it by showing godly knowledge, righteousness, and holiness (Col. 3:10; Eph. 4:24). It's an awesome thing to consider that every time you act kindly toward an irritating person, you are imaging God. "Image" is a verb as well as a noun. It's something we do as well as something we have.

Third, we image God by conforming to Jesus Christ in suffering and death, the ultimate examples of self-giving love. I'll say much more about this in the section on redemption. For now, it's enough to see that God responds to evil with justice and compassion, and both lead God voluntarily to undertake suffering "for us and for our salvation."[20] Because the Son of God became "a man of suffering" (Isa. 53:3), we who image God will suffer too. Because the Son of God dies, so must those who hope, like him, to be raised to new life. The disciple is not greater than his master. In both cases, she who loses her life shall find it; he who is humbled will be exalted; the one who dies shall live.

The Meaning of the Christian Doctrine of Creation

It's characteristic of Reformed and many other Christians (perhaps especially Catholics) to say a lot about creation, to speak of it with enthusiasm, and to think hard about its meaning and implications for scholarship and life more generally. Let's ponder eight of these deeper meanings, bearing in mind that each will form a thread that can be

---

20. The Nicene Creed's statement of the purpose of the incarnation.

followed through the drama of the fall and redemption, and, in some cases, clear through to the consummation of history in "the new heaven and new earth."

First, the original goodness of creation implies that all of it, including any human being we meet, is potentially redeemable. Just as a banged-up, badly repaired, out-of-tune Stradivarius violin would still be unmistakable to a trained eye and ear, so everything made by God retains at least some part of its goodness and promise. It has come from the shop of a master. This is true of polluted forest streams, and it is also true of polluted minds and hearts. Because of corruption, no human being is as good as he can be; but, because of the strength of creation and of God's faithfulness in preserving it, no human being is as bad as he could be either. (Bank robbers, for instance, are sometimes kind to their mothers.)

Second, created things — and their parts and processes — are unique and sometimes mysterious, but because they have come from the wisdom of God they are also purposive and, in principle, intelligible.[21] As we'll see in the next section, Christians know that creation and our understanding of it have been corrupted. Some of what we see in creation looks cold, remote, hostile, and bloody. The world has become "disenchanted" for us. But, again, because of the built-in strength of creation and because of God's preservation of its main features, human beings have reason to study creation in hope of learning its nature. Christians who have Scripture as a lens for viewing the world, as Calvin said, can also hope to learn something of the nature of the Creator, including his power, imagination, and sheer intelligence.

Calvin adds that the creation, read through the special revelation of Scripture, tells us of God's goodness. The rich abundance and variety of created goods, in particular, tell us that God is out to please his creatures. Calvin could have mentioned sunsets or moonbeams in this connection, but, because he was French, Calvin mentions food,

21. Langdon Gilkey, *Maker of Heaven and Earth: A Study of the Christian Doctrine of Creation* (Garden City, NY: Doubleday, 1959), 55.

wine, and flowers.[22] He observes that the earth's abundance of fruits isn't strictly necessary to sustain animal and human life. Calvin's idea appears to be that, given apples, we could probably have gotten along without pears, for example. But variety delights us (and, for all we know, maybe it delights animals too). So it's God's goodness we have to thank for imagining and providing fruits as different from each other as a banana and a plum.

Third, God created the heavens and the earth out of his own goodness, power, and love — out of his own enthusiasm for being. So when the church's confessions say that "out of nothing" God "created heaven and earth and everything in them,"[23] what this means is that God used no preexisting forms or materials distinct from his own mind. God wasn't "limited by his medium." He had no monster to subdue, no "givens with which he had to work." Nothing precedes God or constitutes a true rival for God. God is the absolute originator, bringing finite existence into reality from nothing but his own sovereign imagination and grace.[24]

What follows is that even though we can spot signs of God everywhere, God and the world are really distinct. The world is not a piece of God or a part of God. It's not God's "double" or "alter ego."[25] Christians who accept that God created the world therefore reject pantheism in its various forms. According to pantheism (the word means, roughly, "all is God"), everything in the universe is one thing or the manifestation of one thing, and this one thing is worthy of worship. Call it "God-world." Spiritualist pantheists say of everything that it is God or part of God. Materialist pantheists say of everything that it is the world or part of the world.

The trouble with spiritual pantheism is that it is behind the

22. David Steinmetz, "The Intellectual Appeal of the Reformation" (unpublished ms., Princeton, 1999), 4, commenting on Calvin, *Institutes,* 1:720 (3.10.2).

23. The Heidelberg Catechism, Answer 26, commenting on the first article of the Apostles' Creed: "I believe in God the Father almighty, creator of heaven and earth."

24. Gilkey, *Maker of Heaven and Earth,* 52-53.

25. Emil Brunner, *Dogmatics,* 3 vols. (Philadelphia: Westminster, 1949-62), vol. 2: *The Christian Doctrine of Creation and Redemption,* trans. Olive Wyon, 4.

times. It was once true that everything in the universe was God, but that was before creation.[26] We now have both an infinite God and a finite world, and it is important not to confuse them. Materialist pantheists, on the other hand, have difficulty distinguishing themselves from atheists. Expectably, the most enthusiastic of them — the ones who truly love the material world — also court idolatry. They tend to worship the creature rather than the Creator (Rom. 1:25), succumbing to the oldest temptation of all.

Fourth, St. Francis of Assisi and his kin show us how to love the natural world without worshiping it. In their eyes, material reality is a good thing. God loves matter, which is why he made lots of it (God must love space even more). Moreover, God made human beings to be embodied creatures, and the second person of God honored us by assuming our flesh and blood. Every Christian hopes for "the resurrection of the body" so that in the life everlasting we may learn some bodily moves we never had earthly time for, such as the backstroke and the Texas two-step. The reason this is possible is that the "new heaven and new earth" is apparently going to be a physical setting with physical joys, such as eating and drinking with Jesus (Matt. 26:29).

It follows that the things of the mind and spirit are no better, and are sometimes much worse, than the things of the body. Christianity rejects those "boutique spiritualities," ancient and modern, that scorn the messy, organic nature of physical life. The human spirit is not necessarily more aristocratic than the human body.[27] It is not more Christian to play chess than to play hockey. It is not more Christian to become a minister than to become a muck farmer.

It's true that material things and events sometimes hurt us, but not necessarily because they are evil. St. Paul states that creation is now "in bondage to decay" (Rom. 8:21), but that doesn't mean that every "natural disaster" may be attributed to nature's decadence.

---

26. C. S. Lewis, *The Problem of Pain* (New York: Macmillan, 1962), 150.
27. Eugene H. Peterson, "Christ Plays in Ten Thousand Places, I: The Play of Creation," *Perspectives,* June/July 2000, 8.

Some of these disasters have a human component. For various reasons, some foolish and some tragic, human beings sometimes put themselves in harm's way where nature is concerned, building houses in known hurricane alleys, for example, or on flood plains, or along dry timber ridges. The wind, water, or fire that harms such people in such places is not necessarily out of bounds. When such forces hurt us, it might be because we are out of bounds.

> *"It is not only prayer that gives God glory but work. Smiting on an anvil, sawing a beam, whitewashing a wall, driving horses, sweeping, scouring, everything gives God some glory if being in his grace you do it as your duty. To go to communion worthily gives God great glory, but a man with a dungfork in his hand, a woman with a sloppail, give him glory too. He is so great that all things give him glory if you mean they should."*
>
> Gerard Manley Hopkins[28]

Fifth, in Genesis God affirms the goodness of work and of marriage — the ordinary means of production and reproduction — with the repeated affirmation that "he saw that it was good" or even "very good." In fact, as we have seen, God gave the primal pair of human beings a cultural mandate (or blessing) to multiply and to fill the earth, to care for it, to work with it (Gen. 1:26-28). This is the positive reason

---

28. Gerard Manley Hopkins, from "The Principle or Foundation," an address based on *The Spiritual Exercises of St. Ignatius Loyola,* in *Ordinary Graces: Christian Teachings on the Interior Life,* ed. Lorraine Kisly with an intro. by Philip Zalieski (New York: Bell Tower, 2000), 170.

for the sixteenth-century Protestant affirmation of ordinary life and culture, that is, of the normal practices of human hands and minds — an affirmation shared by modern Catholics.[29] We needn't become priests or nuns in order to have a vocation, and we needn't withdraw to monasteries in order to serve God maximally. As we'll see in Chapter 5, work and play, friendship and marriage, business and art (probably even government) are all intrinsically good things and may all have a part in a Christian's vocation. God has "hallowed" these good things and has called us to relish and employ them. A slice of bread or a game of soccer may tell us of God's goodness as surely, even if not as directly, as a tract, and this is true even if the baker and the player do not realize that their activity has been sponsored by God. The Christian at her drafting board may be engaged in "full-time Christian service" as surely as the priest at his altar. Prayer is a holy offering to God, but so is work. In fact, according to an old Christian epigram, work *is* prayer. (Many of us know that thoughtful prayer is also work.) Celibacy is a valid Christian option, but so is marriage. The Genesis affirmations by God — This is good! This is *very* good! — reveal God's enthusiasm for life in all its variety and abundance, suggesting that it might be healthy for us to follow suit with some enthusiasm of our own.

Sixth, the declaration "Let us create humankind in our image" implies a range of human responsibilities, including those associated with earthkeeping and creativity. But it also secures a range of human rights, including the right to respect, the right to life, and the right to certain freedoms. These are unalienable rights. No human being has granted them, and none may remove them. Personhood is not an achievement, but a given. The same is true of our dignity — the natural weightiness and worthiness of creatures designed to look like God. A person with dignity has a low center of gravity and is hard to topple. In an often-quoted passage, C. S. Lewis speculates on this "weight of glory" in each of our neighbors:

29. Charles Taylor, *Sources of the Self: The Making of the Modern Identity* (Cambridge, MA: Harvard University Press, 1989), 216-27.

It is a serious thing to live in a society of possible gods and god-
desses, to remember that the dullest and most uninteresting
person you can talk to may one day be a creature which, if you
saw it now, you would be strongly tempted to worship, or else a
horror or a corruption such as you now meet, if at all, only in a
nightmare. All day long we are, in some degree, helping each
other to one or other of these destinations. There are no *ordinary* people. You have never talked to a mere mortal.[30]

Seventh, the fact that individual human beings, and also the holy
catholic church, have been created in the image of God implies the
need to balance our individual and corporate identities. Each of us is
unrepeatable, a unique bearer and reflector of the glory of God. Nobody else can reflect God's light in exactly the same way as you can.
But none of us is an *independent* person. We live in a web of dependen-
cies, not only on God, but also on a world of people, including people
who preceded us. (Even rebels depend in numerous ways on the culture they protest.)[31] Our dual status is especially clear within the
Christian church, which St. Paul compares to a body comprising
many parts or members, each unique, but each necessary too, and all
required to mesh well with the others in order for the body to do its
work (1 Cor. 12). The fact is that we are distinct persons created for
communion, and we are a communion created to honor personal differences.

What follows within a Christian community is that we'll need to
welcome, even enfold each other, while also honoring each other's pri-
vacy. Learning to do this may require painful experience, and we get
some of it in residence hall living in the first year of college. Unfortu-
nately, experience is a hard teacher: she tests us first and gives the lesson later.

Eighth, the Christian doctrine of creation *places* us in the scheme

30. Lewis, "Weight of Glory," 18-19.
31. Jacques Barzun, *From Dawn to Decadence, 1500 to the Present: 500 Years of Western
Cultural Life* (New York: HarperCollins, 2000), xiii.

of things. We are not God, but only *images* of God. On the other hand, we are images of *God,* and not mere products of natural selection working off random genetic mutation. Christians therefore reject both materialist reduction of our status and humanist exaggeration of it. Christians reject the "nothing but" philosophies in which our humanity — including our loves and hates, our morality, religion, nostalgia, and hope — is nothing but a product of blind, unsupervised evolutionary development and consists in nothing but chemical and electronic systems and events. Christians reject reductionist accounts of human love, for example, that describe it solely in terms of survival value. Given the possibility that we may enjoy union with Christ in the "intermediate state" between our death and the general resurrection at the end of the age (Phil. 1:21-24; 2 Cor. 5:6-9), most Christians reject the claim that we are nothing but our bodies.

In sum, against any materialist reductionism, Christians claim that God has seen fit to make room in the universe for creatures who bear some of the glory of their Maker, and who, even on the rainiest Monday morning of their lives, look something like God. We image God in our personhood, communion, responsibility, dignity, virtue, suffering, and freedom.

But, against humanist exaltation of our status, we need to recall that our freedom is relative, that our personhood is derivative, that everything important about us is ultimately God's gift. We need to recall that wisdom's first child is humility, and that humility means a kind of realism about our place in the scheme of things so that we don't end up thinking of ourselves more highly than we ought to think (Rom. 12:3).

We need these sobering recollections in a world of humanist and "creative anti-realist" claims. While naturalists claim that we have come from nature, creative anti-realists claim that nature has, in important ways, come from us. That is, creative anti-realists think that our minds impose on reality its very character and structure, so that if our minds weren't at work there simply wouldn't be any of the things we experience each day. According to this philosophy, we create by our choosing, or by our thinking, or by our speaking. The general idea (pioneered by the philosopher Immanuel Kant on one reading of this complex thinker) is that it is not our minds that must conform to reality; instead, reality must conform to our minds.[32]

According to creative anti-realists, we create ourselves too — and periodically re-create ourselves. We generate ourselves out of our own minds, and we keep on regenerating ourselves into wholly new persons. The American philosopher Richard Rorty thinks that we can create these new selves by redescribing ourselves. Instead of accepting a self-description from Scripture or confession, let's say, we may reinvent ourselves in the manner of "strong poets," who believe that human nature is to be made, not discovered. According to Rorty, "we hope by this continual re-description to make the best selves for ourselves that we can."[33] (These periodic reinventions of ourselves come in handy when we are expected to keep a promise made by one of our old selves.)

The trouble with this perspective is that, with all of us human creators at work, it looks as if we have as many worlds as there are people, or as many worlds as there are cultures. We all construct *different* worlds. According to creative anti-realism, there isn't any "way things are." There is only the way you think things are, and the way I do. There is only the way one culture thinks things are, and the way every other culture does. According to this kind of relativism, what's true is what's "true for you," and what's true is also what's "true for me." Both truths are true, even if they conflict.[34]

What may we say about creative anti-realism and about the postmodern way of thinking it expresses? On the one hand, Christians must concede that we do see reality from our own points of view conditioned by a hundred features of our own lives, personal and cultural. We do sometimes see only appearances, not realities. Worse, our claims to knowledge of reality do sometimes mask a hidden agenda

32. Alvin Plantinga, "The Twin Pillars of Christian Scholarship," The Stob Lectures, 1989-90 (Grand Rapids: Calvin College, 1990), 14-17.

33. Rorty, *Contingency, Irony, and Solidarity* (Cambridge: Cambridge University Press, 1989), 80.

34. Plantinga, "The Twin Pillars," 18.

that has our own arrogance mixed up in it somewhere. These sad facts should make Christians modest in claiming to know exactly how things are in the world. After all, our thinking is frequently marred by error and sometimes by serious self-deception.

On the other hand, that very fact should stop us from supposing that whatever we believe is true, that we construct reality by thinking about it, as if the truth is whatever I think it is. Not at all. That's true only of God. God created the heavens and the earth, including us. What follows is that there really is "a way things are," and this is so even if God is the only being in the universe who knows this state of affairs exactly. What also follows is that some things are objectively true: they are true no matter what anybody thinks of them. It is objectively true, for example, that kindness is better than cruelty even if cruel people think of things the other way around. It is objectively true that "in Christ, God was reconciling the world to himself" (2 Cor. 5:19) even if some people don't believe it. It's objectively true that millions of people perished under the rule of Adolf Hitler, even though deniers of the Holocaust claim that this story is mostly myth and exaggeration.

To have a creation — something with both deep structures and also continuous change and process — is to have a place that is both stable and dynamic. In a creation of this kind we may make enduring commitments, confident that God's handiwork is anchored into *God's* enduring commitments. Among other advantages, this lets us do science with the expectation of regular, predictable patterns in creation, even regular patterns of dynamic change. True, we have to allow for the possibility of miraculous acts of God, and therefore we can't expect sheer uniformity in our experience of creation. God (or one of God's authorized deputies) does sometimes act extraordinarily for particular redemptive purposes. But we may nonetheless expect regularity within creation and its phenomena, a stable platform for living and learning. We can have science because our daily experience is so unlike the hypothetical situation once imagined by the philosopher Ludwig Wittgenstein: What if we saw "houses gradually turning into steam without any obvious cause; if the cattle in the fields stood on their heads and laughed and spoke comprehensible words; if trees gradually turned into men and men into trees"?[35]

To sum up, the first act in the world's drama is God's act of creating and sustaining "all things visible and invisible,"[36] out of a generous desire to enlarge the realm of being, to bestow life and goodness on others, and to assist others to flourish in the realm created for them.

35. Wittgenstein, *On Certainty*, ed. G. E. M. Anscombe and G. H. von Wright (Oxford: Basil Blackwell, 1969), sect. 12.4, par. 513.
36. The Nicene Creed.

The Fall

*The man said, "The woman whom you gave to be with me,
she gave me fruit from the tree, and I ate." . . . The woman
said, "The serpent tricked me, and I ate."*

Genesis 3:12-13

*Fools say in their hearts, "There is no God."
They are corrupt, . . .
. . . they are all alike perverse.*

Psalm 14:1, 3

They have turned their backs to me, and not their faces.

Jeremiah 2:27

*They became futile in their thinking, and their senseless
minds were darkened.*

Romans 1:21

*I do not understand my own actions. For I do not do what I
want, but I do the very thing I hate.*

Romans 7:15

The creation was subjected to futility.

Romans 8:20

G od's original judgment on creation was that it was "good," even "very good." God made a paradise, and we can still find signs of it. Christians can still sing "This Is My Father's World" and do it with gusto:

This is my Father's world, and to my listening ears
All nature sings, and round me rings the music
 of the spheres. . . .
This is my Father's world: he shines in all that's fair;
In rustling grass I hear him pass — he speaks
 to me everywhere.

It's a good hymn, but it gives us only half the picture — only paradise, and not paradise lost. As matters stand, creation still declares the glory of God, but it also declares the tragedy of fallenness, of

> "Formlessness is . . . neither civilized nor natural. It is a peculiarly human evil, without analogue in nature, caused by the failures of civilization: inattention, irresponsibility, carelessness, ignorance of consequence. It is the result of the misuse of power."
>
> Wendell Berry[1]

chaos, of painful carnivorousness. On a bluebird day in May, "all nature sings and round me rings," and you can probably recall a few bluebird days that had some longing and delight in them. But nature

1. Wendell Berry, "The Specialization of Poetry," in *The Poet's Work*, ed. Reginald Gibbons (Boston: Houghton Mifflin, 1979), 147.

also includes animals that tear each other up and animals that rape each other or kill each other for sport. Some animal parents devour their own offspring. Creation speaks out of both sides of its mouth now. It still sings and rings, but it also groans. As Paul says, "the whole creation has been groaning" for release from its "bondage to decay" (Rom. 8:21-22).

The whole creation includes us. To see human decay, all you have to do is look around town, look around the world. You'll find both hostility and indifference. In fact, you'll find hostility packaged as entertainment and indifference treated as normal. (In Scripture it's just as evil, and perhaps more common, to turn one's back on God or neighbor as to attack them.) Every day's news shows us a new assortment of merciless dictators, negligent contractors, remorseless killers. Year after year we see new film footage of old miseries — for example, of refugees forced out of their houses and onto long marches by soldiers who are "simply following orders" in conflicts fueled by long memories and short tempers. As others have noticed, human depravity is the one part of Christian doctrine that can be *proved*.

Human depravity was made all too clear on Tuesday, September 11, 2001, when the whole world looked into the face of evil. The terrorists who flew airliners into New York's World Trade Center and Washington's Pentagon planned the attacks for maximum death and destruction, not only to those who fell under direct assault, but also to the spirit of a watching Western world, forced to see spectacular images of its own vulnerability. Words like "wickedness" seemed suddenly resonant again as the world's acoustics changed in a single day.

Philosophers have long pondered the human condition, and they have noticed that evil is the main human problem. Even when these thinkers reject God, they recognize that the world is out of joint and that human beings, too, are "alienated," or "divided," or "repressed." Human beings live irrationally, as philosophers put it, or "inauthentically." The philosopher Arthur Schopenhauer described the human condition in a particularly bleak way. "If we want to know what people are worth morally," said Schopenhauer, "we have only to consider their fate as a whole and in general. This is want, wretchedness, affliction, misery, and death."[2]

Human life is not the way it's supposed to be. And so, as we saw earlier, the world's great thinkers often diagnose the human predicament and prescribe various remedies for it. They diagnose ignorance and prescribe education. They diagnose oppression and prescribe justice. They diagnose the conformism of "bad faith" and prescribe the freedom of authentic choice. A few look at the world, fall into a depression, and put their prescription pad away.

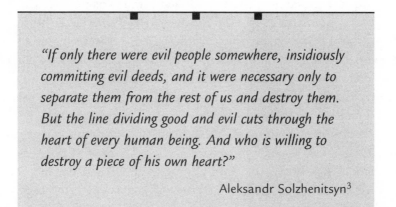

"If only there were evil people somewhere, insidiously committing evil deeds, and it were necessary only to separate them from the rest of us and destroy them. But the line dividing good and evil cuts through the heart of every human being. And who is willing to destroy a piece of his own heart?"

Aleksandr Solzhenitsyn[3]

Christians think that the usual diagnoses and prescriptions catch part of the truth, but that they do not get to the bottom of it. The human problem isn't just ignorance; it's also stubborn pride. It's not just oppression; it's also corruption. That's why newly liberated victims of oppression often end up oppressing others. The human prob-

2. Schopenhauer, *The World as Will and Idea* (London: Everyman, 1995), 216.

3. Aleksandr Solzhenitsyn, quoted in Fred E. Katz, *Ordinary People and Extraordinary Evil: A Report on the Beguilings of Evil* (New York: New York State University Press, 1993), vii. For this quote, I am indebted to Quentin J. Schultze, *Communicating for Life: Christian Stewardship in Community and Media* (Grand Rapids: Baker Book House/ BakerAcademic, 2000), 38.

lem isn't just that we timidly conform to prevailing modes of life; it's also that nothing human can jolt us out of our slump. Even a move to a pristine backwoods in British Columbia won't save us because we carry our trouble with us.

The real human predicament, as Scripture reveals, is that inexplicably, irrationally, we all keep living our lives against what's good for us. In what can only be called the mystery of iniquity, human beings from the time of Adam and Eve (and, before them, a certain number of angelic beings) have so often chosen to live against God, against each other, and against God's world. We live even against ourselves. An addict, for example, partakes of a substance or practice that he knows might kill him. For a time he does so freely. He has a choice. He freely starts a "conversion unto death," and, for reasons he can't fully explain, he doesn't stop until he crashes.[4] He starts out with a choice. He ends up with a habit. And the habit slowly converts to a kind of slavery that can be broken only by God or, as they say in the twelve-step literature, "a higher power."

According to Genesis 3 and Romans 5, our whole race "has a habit" where sin is concerned. Near the beginning of our history, we human beings broke the harmony of paradise and began to live against our ultimate good, our *summum bonum*. As Genesis 3 and Genesis 4 reveal, we rebelled against God and then we fled from God. We once had a choice. We now have a near-compulsion — at least, that's what we have without the grace of God to set us free. Over the centuries we humans have ironed in this near-compulsion, with the result that each new generation enters a world that has long ago lost its Eden, a world that is now half-ruined by the billions of bad choices and millions of old habits congealed into thousands of cultures across all the ages. In this world even saints discover, in exasperation, that whenever they want to do right "evil lies close at hand" (Rom. 7:21). We are "conceived and born in sin," as Calvinists sometimes put it when they baptize an infant. This is a way of stating the doctrine of original sin, that is, that the corruption and guilt of our first parents

---

4. Patrick McCormick, *Sin as Addiction* (New York: Paulist, 1989), 152.

have run right down the generations, tainting us all. As the author Garry Wills writes, none of us has a fresh start:

> We are hostages to each other in a deadly interrelatedness. There is no "clean slate" of nature unscribbled on by all one's forebears. . . . At one time a woman of unsavory enough experience was delicately but cruelly referred to as "having a past." The doctrine of original sin states that humankind, in exactly that sense, "has a past."[5]

Evil is what's wrong with the world, and it includes trouble in nature as well as in human nature. It includes disease as well as theft, birth defects as well as character defects. We might define evil as *any spoiling of shalom,* any deviation from the way God wants things to be. Thinking along these lines, we can see that sin is a subset of evil: it's any evil for which somebody is to blame, whether as an individual or as a member of a group. All sin is evil, but not all evil is sin. A killing by a two-year-old who picks up a gun is a terrible evil, but not an actual sin, at least not by the two-year-old. But a premeditated killing by a drug dealer of a drug enforcement officer is both evil and sinful. So is willful ignorance and silence about the evils perpetrated by one's own nation. In short, sin is *culpable evil.*

God hates sin not just because it violates law, but also because it violates trust. Sin grieves God, offends God, betrays God, and not because God is touchy. God hates sin against himself, against neighbors, against a good creation, because sin breaks the peace — in the first place between the sinner and God. Sin interferes with the way God wants things to be. That is why God has laws against it. God is for shalom and *therefore* against sin.

Because sin spoils the way things are supposed to be, biblical images for sin suggest that it is deviant behavior. In the Bible, to sin is to miss the target, to wander from the path, to stray from the fold. A sin-

5. Wills, *Reagan's America: Innocents at Home* (Garden City, NY: Doubleday, 1987), 384.

ner has a deaf ear or a stiff neck. To sin is to overstep a line or else to fail to reach it; that is, sin is either transgression or shortcoming. These and other images tell us that, in a biblical view of the world, sin is a familiar, even predictable, part of life, but it is not normal. And the fact that "everybody does it" doesn't *make* it normal.

Given its source in God, goodness is original, normal, constructive. Evil is secondary, abnormal, destructive. In fact, evil needs good in order to be evil. As C. S. Lewis wrote, "a cow cannot be very good or very bad; a dog can be both better and worse; a child better and worse still; an ordinary [person], still more so; a [person] of genius still more so; a superhuman spirit best — or worst — of all." Why is this so? Because "the better stuff a creature is made of — the cleverer and stronger and freer it is — then the better it will be if it goes right, but also the worse it will be if it goes wrong."[6]

Here we can see that evil is a kind of parasite on goodness. The intelligence of Nazi commanders came from God. The truth portion of an effective lie (maybe 90 percent of it) makes the lie plausible. The physical power of a guilty assailant comes from the gift of good health. Badness can't be very bad without tapping deeply into goodness. Badness is twisted goodness, polluted goodness, divided goodness. But even after the twisting, polluting, and dividing have happened, the goodness is still there.

According to Genesis 3, sin appeared very early in the history of our race. In this chapter our first parents try to be "like God, knowing good and evil," and succeed only in alienating themselves from God and from each other. They choose to believe the tempter rather than their Maker and turn their garden into a bramble patch. The good and fruitful earth becomes their foe (Gen. 3:17-18; cf. 4:12-14), and their own sin then rises in a terrible crescendo. Adam and Eve's pride and disbelief trigger revolt, scapegoating, and flight from God (Gen. 3:4-5, 10, 12-13). Their first child ups the ante: Cain resents and kills his brother Abel, launching the history of envy that leads to murder. Like his parents and the rest of the race, Cain refuses to face his sin

---

6. C. S. Lewis, *Mere Christianity* (New York: Macmillan, 1960), 53.

("Am I my brother's keeper?") and is exiled by God to a place "east of Eden." In a phrase that suggests the restlessness of all who are alienated from God, Cain becomes "a fugitive and a wanderer on the earth," a murderer who now fears other murderers and has to be protected from them by a mysterious mark that God places upon him.

Among these strangers (Genesis hasn't the slightest interest in telling us where they came from) Cain starts a family and passes sin down the generations like a gene. At the sixth generation, the Genesis narrator pauses to snap a picture of a homicidal braggart by the name of Lamech.

> You wives of Lamech, listen. . . .
> I have killed a man for wounding me,
>   a young man for striking me.
> If Cain is avenged sevenfold,
>   truly Lamech seventy-sevenfold.   (Gen. 4:23-24)

From there, the history of sin and corruption moves on, down the ages, in a cast of billions. Each new generation, and each new person, reaps what others have sown and then sows what others will reap. This is true not only of goodness (much-loved children can offer a sense of security to their own spouses and children) but also of evil, which each generation not only receives but also ratifies by its own sin. Terrorists, for example, do not think of themselves as others think of them — irrational zealots consumed by some nameless malice that has turned them into enemies of the peace established by decent people. Like Lamech, they think of their violence as retaliation.[7] And because they have long memories, terrorists may think of themselves as redressing grievances that are decades or even centuries old.

The glory of God's good creation has not been obliterated by the tragedy of the fall, but it has been deeply shadowed by it. The history of our race is, in large part, the interplay of this light and shadow.

7. James T. Burtchaell, *The Giving and Taking of Life: Essays Ethical* (Notre Dame, IN: University of Notre Dame, 1989), 219-20.

Corruption

Measuring the damage of the fall, the Belgic Confession states that by our original sin we human beings have "separated ourselves from God, who is our true life" and have "corrupted our entire nature" (article 14). The Confession means to tie all of us in with Adam, Eve, Cain, and Lamech as their descendants. The first sin of Adam and Eve has spread and congealed into *original sin* — a tendency of the whole race, for which we bear collective guilt. All of us are now bent toward sin. We have in the world not just sins, but sin; not just wrong acts, but also wrong tendencies, habits, practices, and patterns that break down the integrity of persons, families, and whole cultures.

> *"O Lord, thou hast set up many candlesticks, and kindled many lamps in me, but I have either blown them out, or carried them to guide me in forbidden ways."*
>
> John Donne[8]

What are the ingredients in corruption? First, a corrupted person turns God's gifts away from their intended purpose. She *perverts* these gifts. For example, she might use her excellent mind and first-class education not to extend the reach of God's kingdom, but just to get rich. She wants to get rich not in order to support terrific projects in the world, but just to move up the social ladder. We ordinarily think of a prostitute as someone who rents her body. But a person can also rent her mind for a high hourly rate, and she perverts it if she rents it

8. John Donne, from *Essays in Divinity*, in *Ordinary Graces: Christian Teachings on the Interior Life*, ed. Lorraine Kisly with an intro. by Philip Zalieski (New York: Bell Tower, 2000), 75.

because she wants to feel superior to the people who bag her groceries and park her car.

Second, a corrupted person joins together what God has put asunder. He *pollutes* his relationships with foreign elements that don't belong in them. We all know that it's possible to pollute a river by dumping toxic waste into it. But it's also possible to pollute our minds with things that debase them. It's possible to pollute worship by bringing into it unredeemed elements from Vegas lounge shows (the special music is done by a Christian performing artist lying on *top* of the piano). It's possible to pollute friendships with social ambition and college sports with taunting. Good things have a kind of integrity, a kind of oneness or "this-ness." A polluted event or relationship is one that has been compromised by introducing into it something that doesn't belong there. Now the event or relationship isn't just "this," but "this and that."

> "We have plenty of examples in this world of poor things being used for good purposes. God can make any indifferent thing, as well as evil itself, an instrument for good; but I submit that to do this is the business of God and not of any human being."
>
> Flannery O'Connor[9]

Take the case of idolatry. Like an adulterer, an idolater corrupts a relationship by introducing a third party into it. (In Scripture, idolatry and adultery are often paired up as emblems of each other.) So idolatry isn't just an act of craving fame, for example, instead of God.

9. Flannery O'Connor, *Mystery and Manners* (New York: Farrar, Straus & Giroux, 1969), 174.

Idolatry is also the act of putting fame *alongside* God and trying to serve them both. Your god, said Martin Luther, is "whatever your heart clings to," and that often means we've got more than one god. We are like an adulterous husband who, right through his affair, "still loves his wife." He loves two women, or so he thinks. Similarly, a Christian who wants to be God's child, but also wants to be famous and admired in the world, is a person with two loves. God and fame. Fame and God. He loves them both. He "wants it all."

In Scripture God warns against double-mindedness of this kind, not only because it is disloyal, not only because it is staggeringly ungrateful to our Maker and Savior, but also because it is so foolish. Idols can't take the weight we put on them; they're *false* gods. Worldly fame can occasionally be used to gain a hearing for the gospel, but it cannot forgive us. It can't cure us. Despite rumors, it can't secure us. And the untamed desire for it can split a person. Divided worship splits worshipers. Divided love splits lovers. The truth is, we have to choose. Like a sailor with one foot on a dock and the other on a departing catamaran, we have to choose.

The Bible's account of the human predicament is that from the start we've been choosing wrong. We've kept on perverting and polluting God's gifts. It's not just that each of us commits individual sins — telling lies, for example, or wasting time. The situation is much more serious than this. By sinning we not only grieve God and our neighbor; we also wreck our own integrity. We are like people whose abuse of alcohol ruins not only their liver but also their judgment and will, the things that might have kept them from further abuse of alcohol. The same pattern holds for everybody. We now sin because we are sinners, because we have a habit, and because the habit has damaged our judgment and will.

I think we understand how this process works. A woman who has gotten into the habit of lying might eventually find it hard to tell the difference between a lie and the truth. Whatever's convenient seems "true" to her. She now lies because she's a liar. And she has no particular desire to change. Similarly, a man who thinks women are "broads" might feel insulted — and angry — when a woman refuses to be treated like a broad. The reason is that he feels entitled to his sexism, and he feels sure that she isn't entitled to object to it. His sexism has corrupted his judgment.

When we sin we corrupt ourselves, but we may corrupt others too. A father who beats up his son breaks some of the bones of self-respect that hold his son's character together. As the novelist Russell Banks shows in *Affliction* (maybe you've seen the masterful film by Paul Schrader that's based on it), an abusive father might break down his son's dignity to such an extent as to wreck his son's chances of making and keeping solid relationships. In fact, abuse fosters abuse, or, as social scientists say, abuse predicts abuse. Victims victimize others, and even themselves. In this way sin gains momentum. Worse, all sinful lives intersect with other sinful lives — in families, businesses, educational and political institutions, churches, social clubs, and so forth — in such a way that the progress of both good and evil looks like wave after wave of intertwined spirals.

Where the waves meet, cultures form. In a racist culture, racism will look normal. In a secular culture, indifference toward God will look normal, as it does in much secular education. Human character forms culture, but culture also forms human character. And the formation runs not only across regions and peoples but also along generations. A boy can "inherit" his father's sexist idea that men ought to dominate women. A daughter can "inherit" her mother's sexist idea that women ought to let men do it.

The result of all this spiraling and inheriting is devastating. Whole matrices of evil appear in which various forms of wrongdoing cross-pollinate and breed. The "gaming" culture, for example, includes a lot more than slot machines and roulette tables: it also partners with the sex, liquor, and pawn shop industries to foster multiple addictions. The culture of war includes not only killing, its main business, but also such side businesses as espionage, counterespionage, treachery, disinformation, profiteering, prostitution, and drug abuse. "War is hell," not only because of its violence and destruction, but also because of the physically and morally nauseating atmosphere it generates. Popular entertainment culture includes not only songs and dances, but also films that glorify greed or mindless chauvinism and that routinely portray the parents of teenagers as naive or stupid.

When we are born into the world, we are born into these matrices and atmospheres. Our slate has been scribbled on by others. We are born into a world in which, for centuries, sin has damaged the great interactive network of shalom — snapping or twisting the thousands of bonds that give particular beings integrity and that tie them to others.

Corruption is thus a *dynamic* motif in the Christian understanding of sin: it is not so much a particular sin as the multiplying power of all sin to spoil a good creation and to breach its defenses against invaders. We might describe corruption as spiritual AIDS — a systemic and progressive devastation of our spiritual immune system that eventually breaks it down and opens the way for hordes of opportunistic sins. These make life progressively miserable: conceit, for instance, typically generates envy of rivals, a nasty form of resentment that eats away at the one who envies. "Sin," as Augustine says, "becomes the punishment of sin."[10]

All this corruption amounts to a pervasive depravity of human nature, a condition Calvinists have traditionally called "total depravity." This doesn't mean that we are all as nasty as we can be. It doesn't mean that, in a corrupted state, we always choose the worst alternative. Even in a fallen world, ordinary people practice ordinary kindness every day. They build hospitals, organize relief efforts, and manage twelve-step programs for addicts. A warring world that needs peacemakers also has some, and some of the great ones get prizes. The Holy Spirit preserves much of the original goodness of creation and also inspires new forms of goodness — and not only in those people the Spirit has regenerated. Besides such regenerating grace, which actually turns a person's heart back toward God, the Spirit also distributes "common grace," an array of God's gifts that preserves and enhances human life even when not regenerating it. As John Calvin

---

10. Augustine, *On the Merits and Remission of Sins*, 2.36.22: "What is called 'sin' dwelling in our members is sin in this way: that it becomes the punishment of sin." (I owe this reference and translation to Professor Mark F. Williams.)

observes, God's Spirit works everywhere in the world to pour out good gifts on the merciful and the unmerciful, on the grateful and the ungrateful, on believers and unbelievers alike. (Rain falls on the fields of unbelievers, too.) Moreover, God checks the spread of corruption by preserving in humanity a sense of divinity and the voice of conscience. To bridle lawlessness, God uses shame, fear of discovery, fear of the law, even a desire for profit among those who believe that honesty is the best policy. Further, God preserves a basic sense of civic justice — a "seed of political order" to go along with the seed of religion — and, for enrichment of life, invests particular talents in jurists, scientists, artists, and poets.[11] Still further, the world's great religions contain civilizing tendencies, greater or smaller, that remind us of God's will for the kingdom. (Christian peacemakers have learned much from Gandhi.) The same goes for customs and traditions. As I said, culture forms character, and the result may be very bad. But it

> *Common Grace: The goodness of God shown to all, regardless of faith, consisting in natural blessings, restraint of corruption, seeds of religion and political order, and a host of civilizing and humanizing impulses, patterns, and traditions.*

may also be quite good, as one can tell in traditional Asian cultures with low crime rates and high regard for the elderly. Popular U.S. culture, which sometimes celebrates lust and trivializes faith, can also stir us with a call for humanitarian aid, or with a film such as *Dead Man Walking*, which powerfully portrays redemption through confession and forgiveness of sin. Add these things up, and you'll have an

11. Calvin, *Institutes,* 1:43-45 (1.3.1-2), 1:272-73 (2.2.13-14), 1:292-93 (2.3.3).

impressive number of common graces. The Holy Spirit often blows ahead of the progress of the gospel, and to remarkable effect.

According to the doctrine of total depravity, human beings need common grace just to keep life going in relatively civil ways. This is so because evil contaminates everything — minds as well as bodies, churches as well as states, preachers as well as pro wrestlers. People sometimes rebel against grace itself. For example, they might feel insulted to be offered forgiveness, resenting the implication that they need it. Evil runs *through* everything, not around some things.

If you put together the doctrines of common grace and total depravity, you'll be in a position to explain a remarkable fact: worldly people are often better than we expect, and church people are often worse. Church people are sometimes *much* worse than we expect. In fact, says Geoffrey Bromiley, to see sin "in its full range and possibility" we have to look at religious sin, church sin, the kind of sin that people commit ever so piously.[12] It's deeply sobering to reflect on the fact that terrorists who run airliners full of doomed passengers into

> "It's a sad commentary on our world that 'integrity' has slowly been coming to mean self-centeredness. Most people who worry about their integrity are thinking about it in terms of themselves. It's a great excuse for not doing something you really don't want to do, or are afraid to do: 'I can't do that and keep my integrity.' Integrity, like humility, is a quality."
>
> Madeleine L'Engle[13]

12. Geoffrey W. Bromiley, "Sin," in *The International Standard Bible Encyclopedia*, vol. 4, ed. Geoffrey W. Bromiley (Grand Rapids: Eerdmans, 1988), 522.

13. Madeleine L'Engle, *A Circle of Quiet* (New York: Seabury Press, 1972), 130.

populated buildings do it with joyful hearts: they think they're serving the God who will soon reward them as martyrs for righteousness. Satan goes to church more than anybody else because he knows that, at a particular time and place, a corrupt church can devastate the cause of the gospel.

> "The more excellent things are . . . the more manifold will the counterfeits be. So there are perhaps no graces that have more counterfeits than love and humility, these being virtues wherein the beauty of a true Christian does especially appear."
>
> Jonathan Edwards[14]

So what we see, if we look around town, is that it isn't only secularists who "suppress the truth" about God (Rom. 1:18). Believers do it too. How else can we explain that Christians have used their faith to enforce slavery? How else can we explain that Christians have used their faith to suppress honest inquiry into science or history? Or think of this: why does our picture of God so often look like a picture of us? Pondering such questions, Merold Westphal suggests that before we Christians dismiss Marx, Nietzsche, and Freud, the three main architects of "the atheism of suspicion" in the modern age, we ought to learn something from them about the corrupt uses of religion, even of true religion.[15] Honest religious practice builds spiritual momentum: "to those who have, more will be given"; but dishonest religious practice can cause shipwreck in the human soul: "from

14. Jonathan Edwards, *Religious Affections* (1746), ed. John E. Smith (New Haven: Yale University Press, 1959), 146.
15. Westphal, *Suspicion and Faith* (Grand Rapids: Eerdmans, 1993), 13, 16-17.

those who have not, even what they have will be taken away" (Mark 4:25). Aware of this terrible possibility, the Jewish thinker Martin Buber once lamented that just as "there is nothing that can so hide the face of our fellow-man as morality can," so also "religion can hide from us, as nothing else can, the face of God."[16]

Who's to Blame?

But where does all this corruption — including the corruption of religion itself — come from? Could it be that, with some hidden purpose, God causes people to sin? Does the devil make them do it? How about the "powers" that are mentioned, but not really described, in the New Testament (e.g., in Rom. 8:38; Eph. 6:12; Col. 1:16)?

Christians reject these suggestions as classic cases of passing the buck.[17] The first of them (God made me do it) smears the biblical portrait of God: "God is light, and in him there is no darkness at all" (1 John 1:5). God is perfectly holy and therefore hates sin. God outlaws sin, judges it, redeems people from it, forgives it, and suffers to do so. So Christians naturally think it blasphemous to say that God causes anyone to sin. If some "hard saying" of Scripture hints that, to the contrary, God's hands are not wholly clean where sin is concerned — that, for example, in the events preceding the Exodus, God "hardened Pharaoh's heart" — we have to find some way of interpreting such sayings that preserves the portrait of God's holiness. In the case of Pharaoh, we have to notice that the book of Exodus does tell us that Pharaoh's hard heart blocks God's revelation and, for a time, God's rescue attempt. But the text doesn't actually tell us clearly who did the hardening. Did God harden Pharaoh's heart (Exod. 10:1), or did Pharaoh harden his own heart (9:34), or did Pharaoh's heart simply harden all by itself (9:7)? Exodus doesn't answer this question unambiguously.

---

16. Buber, *Between Man and Man*, quoted in Westphal, *Suspicion and Faith*, 25.

17. G. C. Berkouwer, *Sin*, trans. Philip C. Holtrop (Grand Rapids: Eerdmans, 1971), 11-148.

The narrator's interest lies elsewhere, namely, in how God will rescue people when a hard heart is blocking the road out of Egypt.[18]

In the Christian religion God's holiness is strictly nonnegotiable. Not so for the one the New Testament calls Satan or the devil. This is a figure of such power and wiliness that New Testament writers grudgingly title him "the ruler of the demons" (Matt. 12:24) or even "the god of this world" (2 Cor. 4:4). Nonetheless, Satan is no match for Jesus Christ the exorcist, the destroyer of the destroyer. Nor can Satan wreck those who faithfully cling to Christ. Satan can tempt, but not coerce. Satan can accuse, but not convict. Satan can accost, but not destroy — at any rate, cannot destroy those who "put on the whole armor of God" (Eph. 6:11). A central New Testament conviction is that the evil one seduces only those who are in the market for seduction. Satan deceives only the already self-deceived.

In other words (this is the second problem), Satan does not *compel* people to sin. Nor do "the powers," whatever these mysterious things are. Whether they are spirits or forces, whether demons or dynamics (e.g., the power of corruption), whether persons or personifications, whether structures of society or their patterns of influence, mention of "the powers" can cause a shiver of recognition. The reason is that, at some point in our reflection on sin, we come to understand that sin is not only personal but also interpersonal and even suprapersonal. That is, sin is more than the sum of what sinners do. Sin acquires the form of a spirit — the spirit of darkness, the spirit of an age, the spirit of a company or nation. Sin burrows into the bowels of institutions and makes a home there. When this happens, "special interests" bend the law to favor special people like themselves. Whole companies engage in an orgy of deceit. Whole nations join in lockstep with brutal dictators.

No serious Christian wants to claim that the powers rob us of all freedom and accountability, that they *cause* us to sin. In fact, Christians confess that the powers have already been deeply compromised

18. Brevard S. Childs, *The Book of Exodus: A Critical, Theological Commentary* (Philadelphia: Westminster, 1974), 170-75.

by the greater power of God. Don't the victory texts of the New Testament cry out that Jesus Christ has disarmed the powers and principalities, made a spectacle of them, and triumphed over them in such a way that they can never separate believers from the love of God (Col. 2:15; Rom. 8:38-39)?

Still, the powers are aptly named. As the Dutch theologian Hendrikus Berkhof says, mere personal goodness cannot lick them. In fact, their force can seem inevitable.[19]

After all, why *did* millions of ordinary German Christians hand over their lives to Hitler and his band of criminals, thrilling themselves with their new status as members of his movement? Why in the Middle East do neighbors keep turning against each other in a nightmare of hostility? Why do military procurement officials and defense contractors bind themselves into mutually corrupting relationships that cheated taxpayers simply cannot break?

The big systemic evils exasperate us. So many of them seem beyond human reach. They partake of the mystery of iniquity. But, then, so do our personal sins. Why *would* we and others live against God, who is our highest good, the source of our very lives? Why *do* we human beings live against each other, fighting over our cultural differences instead of enjoying them, envying each other's gifts instead of celebrating them? Why *would* we human creatures live against the rest of creation, given its majesty and abundance? *Why would we live against the purpose of our own existence?*[20]

We might say, as Woody Allen did when asked about his affair with his lover's adopted daughter, "the heart wants what it wants." But, of course, that's the problem, not a solution to the problem.

When we come to think about it, the presence of evil in the world poses a number of enduring questions for us. One, as we've just seen, is that people know what's right and still do what's wrong. Another — to return to where we started in this chapter — is the presence of evil

19. Berkhof, *Christian Faith: An Introduction to the Study of the Faith,* trans. Sierd Woudstra (Grand Rapids: Eerdmans, 1979), 208-9.

20. Berkhof, *Christian Faith,* 188.

in nonhuman creation. According to Genesis 3, God cursed the serpent and the earth after human beings fell into sin. Reading this chapter together with Romans 8 (which describes the creation as longing for redemption), Christians have long pondered the extra-human effects of the fall. We are fallen, but so is everything else.

And so we have old questions without good answers: Is carnivorousness a part of God's original design? Judging by the fossil record and by the incisors of carnivores, it seems so. Judging by the scriptural prophecies of shalom and by our own hearts and minds, it seems not so. In Isaiah's picture of God's peaceable kingdom, for example, we find some of the loveliest of all scriptural prophecies, and in them carnivorousness is only a memory:

> The wolf shall live with the lamb,
>   the leopard shall lie down with the kid,
> the calf and the lion and the fatling together,
>   and a little child shall lead them.   (11:6)

The portrait captures our imagination because we wince at the stark realities of "nature red in tooth and claw." If you watch one of those *National Geographic* specials on television in which young lions chase down a deer, leap at its throat or claw their way onto its back, and then start sinking their incisors into the deer's flesh, it all looks more painful than anything we imagine God to delight in.

Here's a place where Christians who read Scripture, read the fossil record, and consult their own sensitivities may come up with more questions than answers. If carnivorousness is part of God's original design, is God less sensitive to animal pain than we are? If not, why do we have what looks like a design for it? Could a pre-fall in the angelic world have anything to do with an answer? Or is that mere speculation? If — actually, in the real world — carnivorousness is one day to cease in the coming of God's peaceable kingdom, how will lions keep up their strength?

I should add that it's no disgrace to have more questions than answers here. It's not even surprising. There is much we don't know about the world, and much we don't know about the meaning of Scripture. Following the Belgic Confession in article 2, Christians who read both the "beautiful book" of the universe (general revelation) and the "holy and divine Word of God" (special revelation) will sometimes find themselves perplexed by the apparent conflict between them, or even within them. A faithful Christian will assume that the conflict *is* only apparent — that God doesn't contradict himself in the two books that reveal him. But she will not assume that we'll be able to resolve the conflict any time soon. Honest, patient scholarship refuses to manage conflicts of these kinds by forcing an early resolution. Instead, the patient Christian scholar puts issues of this kind into suspension for a time while she continues to think about them.

The trouble (this is a third problem) is that if the fallenness of creation extends far and wide, then it extends into our thinking processes themselves. For example, we tend to resist unpalatable truth. We resist the idea that we belong to God and not to ourselves. We resist the idea that our lives themselves have come from God and that we therefore owe God our loyalty and gratitude. We resist these ideas by such devices as willed ignorance and self-deception.

The result, says Calvin, is that we claim to be mere products of nature. Or we pretend to have invented our excellences. We "claim for ourselves what has been given us from heaven."[21] No doubt Calvin means to observe that people often take pride not only in their accomplishments but also in their intelligence, good looks, good breeding, and good coordination, as if they had gifted themselves with these things!

Our thinking has gotten bent, and our learning along with it. Some of Calvin's successors in the Reformed tradition, such as Abraham Kuyper and his interpreters, have thought hard about what it means that our learning has been spoiled by sin. Nicholas Wolterstorff, an eminent Christian philosopher, observes that Kuyper knew a hundred years ago what many know now, namely, that when we try to learn something we bring to the task not only certain "hard-wired capacities for perception, reflection, intellection, and reasoning," but

21. Calvin, *Institutes*, 1:55 (1.5.4).

> *"Nobody ever says, 'I think I will lie to myself today.'*
> *This is the double treachery of self-deception: First we*
> *deceive ourselves, and then we convince ourselves that*
> *we are not deceiving ourselves."*
>
> Lewis Smedes[22]

also mental software formed outside of school, including a whole range of beliefs, assumptions, and commitments.[23] Nobody pursues purely "objective" learning. Everybody pursues "committed" and "socially located" learning. In fact, everybody's learning is "faith-based," and this is so no matter what his scholarly or professional field. The question is never *whether* a person has faith in something or someone, but in *what* or *whom.*

The problem is that we human beings place our faith in nature or in ourselves instead of in God. We identify with our own social group and filter our learning through its membership requirements. So the rich do social science one way and the poor another, and it seems that neither is able to see things from the perspective of the other, and neither even wants to. Or scholars commit to Godlessness, convinced that God would cramp their freedom or intellectual integrity. With remarkable candor, Richard Lewontin, a Harvard biologist, once confessed his faith in materialism:

> Our willingness to accept scientific claims that are against common sense is the key to an understanding of the real struggle between science and the supernatural. We take the side of

22. Lewis B. Smedes, *A Pretty Good Person* (San Francisco: Harper & Row, 1990), 74.

23. Wolterstorff, "Abraham Kuyper on Christian Learning" (unpublished ms., New Haven, 1997), 15-17.

science *in spite* of the patent absurdity of some of its constructs, *in spite* of its failure to fulfill many of its extravagant promises of health and life, *in spite* of the tolerance of the scientific community of unsubstantiated just so stories, because we have a prior commitment, a commitment to materialism. It is not that the methods and institutions of science somehow compel us to accept a material explanation of the phenomenal world, but on the contrary, that we are forced by our a priori adherence to material causes to create an apparatus of investigation and a set of concepts that produce material explanations, no matter how counterintuitive, no matter how mystifying to the uninitiated. Moreover, that materialism is absolute, for we cannot allow a Divine Foot in the door.[24]

It would be hard to find a clearer demonstration of the fact that scholars who believe in God are not the only ones to guide their scholarship by their faith commitment. And atheism at the base of the learning pyramid is only one exhibit of how thinking and learning have gotten bent. People feel estranged from the persons and movements they study, and their estrangement often stems from resentments with a spiritual base. So people form rival schools, with rival systems and worldviews, trying hard not merely to win their way but also to defeat, or even humiliate, somebody from another school. The result is the well-known envy, rivalry, and sheer cussedness of a good deal of the academic enterprise, which is in these ways merely typical of the human enterprise.

Obviously, more education won't fix what's wrong with education. Nor will any other merely human corrective. Such fixes are tainted with the same corruption that needs fixing. That's the bad news. The good news is that God has addressed human corruption from *outside the system,* and it is on this gracious initiative that Christian hope centers.

24. Lewontin, "Billions and Billions of Demons," *The New York Review of Books,* January 7, 1997, 31.

Redemption

4

"*I will establish my covenant between me and you, and your offspring after you throughout their generations . . . to be God to you and to your offspring after you.*"

Genesis 17:7

For to us a child is born,
to us a son is given . . .
and his name will be called
"*Wonderful Counselor, Mighty God,*
Everlasting Father, Prince of Peace."

Isaiah 9:6 (RSV)

But he was wounded for our transgressions,
crushed for our iniquities;
upon him was the punishment that made us whole,
and by his bruises we are healed.

Isaiah 53:5

"*The Lord has risen indeed.*"

Luke 24:34

69

In Christ God was reconciling the world to himself, not counting their trespasses against them.

2 Corinthians 5:19

There is no longer Jew or Greek, there is no longer slave or free, there is no longer male and female; for all of you are one in Christ Jesus.

Galatians 3:28

So if you have been raised with Christ . . . clothe yourselves with compassion, kindness, humility, meekness, and patience.

Colossians 3:1a, 12

Human misery is nearly as old as the human race, but equally old is the story of God's grace, that is, God's mercy to the undeserving. According to Genesis 1 and 2, God had called human beings into fellowship with himself and had blessed them with a world of delights. The fruit of the garden, the companionship of bird and beast, and the joy of love were God's gifts to creatures made in his own image and able to respond to God with gratitude. As we know, the primal pair of human beings risked and lost their estate in a folly of epic proportion, and thus brought upon themselves and their descendants both the judgment and the mercy of God.

In a few words of great sorrow and mystery, Genesis 3 says that after Adam and Eve had disobeyed God "the eyes of both were opened and they knew that they were naked" (v. 7). Their shame was primal, an archetype of the sinner's distress at being exposed. For the first time, human beings had something to hide and something to fear. After the fall, human nakedness began to symbolize not only guilt, and not only exposure to lust. As many people know from dreams, nakedness also began to symbolize vulnerability to ridicule. What fallen people fear is that our threadbare self, with all its deficiencies and deformities, will be undraped before others' eyes, before God's eyes, before our own eyes, and that we will then want the mountains to fall on us and the hills to cover us.

Fallen people can't stand scrutiny. As the theologian Dietrich Bonhoeffer wrote, Adam and Eve couldn't look at each other anymore. They especially had trouble looking into each other's eyes for fear of what they might see there.[1]

But then a wonderful grace note. After the sorry pair of humans has tried to patch themselves up with fig leaves, the narrator tells us that "the LORD God made garments of skins for the man and for his wife, and clothed them" (3:21). Genesis 3 tells us of God's curses on a fallen creation, but in this one verse it also tells us that God cloaks human beings with mercy in a world grown chilly from their own sin.

1. Bonhoeffer, *Ethics,* trans. Neville Horton Smith (New York: Macmillan, 1965), 20.

God outfits human beings with durable clothing they should never have needed — a piece of kindness that launches the history of God's grace from Genesis to Revelation.

Thus Genesis 12 tells of God's call to Abram,[2] and of God's promise not only to him, but also to the whole world. From Abraham's line of people God will make "a great nation," chosen to bless "all the families of the earth" (v. 3). Genesis 15 and 17 then describe God's covenant of grace with Abraham, "an everlasting covenant" that promised a land and a son, Isaac, generated from the barren loins of the aged Abraham and Sarah. God promises above all to attend faithfully to Abraham and to his descendants, "to be God to you and to your offspring after you" (17:7). In a ceremony to ratify the covenant, fire passes between the halves of slain animals (ch. 15), and, in a sign of the covenant, God requires the circumcision of male babies (ch. 17). The mysterious ceremony and sign apparently have to do with the binding solemnity of the covenant, each symbolizing that life and the transmission of life are at stake.

The following stories tell of Isaac and Rebekah, of Hagar and Ishmael, and of a shifty, memorable character by the name of Jacob who one-ups his hairy brother Esau and generally lives his life "strong on guts and weak on conscience" until he is forced to wrestle with God. In a "magnificent defeat" of Jacob's old self at Peniel, God opens the way for Jacob to reconcile with Esau in a ceremony as buoyant with grace as any in Scripture (Gen. 33:1-17).[3] The stories of the patriarchs, matriarchs, and their kin (they are some of the best stories in the Bible) tell of doubt and faith, of strife and reconciliation, of lying and cheating followed by repenting and forgiving. The stories tell how the young nation of Israel ended up in bondage to the Egyptians and how God chose Moses to break Pharaoh's hard heart by leading Israel out of Egypt, through the Red Sea, toward the promised land. Through all these narratives, rich in their detail and intrigue, we hear,

2. Changed to Abraham in Gen. 17:5.

3. Frederick Buechner, *The Magnificent Defeat* (New York: HarperCollins, 1966), 10-18.

as if in the beating of a bass drum, the sound of God's steady commitment to keep covenant with people who break covenant.

> *"What we have lost . . . is a full sense of the power of God — to recruit people who have made terrible choices; to invade the most hopeless lives and fill them with light; to sneak up on people who are thinking about lunch, not God, and smack them up side the head with glory."*
>
> Barbara Brown Taylor[4]

At Mt. Sinai, three months after the Exodus, YHWH (God's holy name, meaning something like "I am the one who is here for you") renews the Genesis covenant of grace, this time with Moses, the mediator of Israel's redemption. Through Moses, the words of God to Israel come laden with love and promise:

> You have seen . . . how I bore you on eagles' wings and brought you to myself. Now therefore, if you obey my voice and keep my covenant, you shall be my treasured possession out of all the peoples. (Exod. 19:4-5)

What God means by "obeying my voice" comes clear when Moses appears out of the fire and smoke of Sinai. Moses emerges with God's Ten Commandments, a set of requirements that people have to fulfill not *in order* to get rescued by God from slavery, but *because* they have been rescued.

4. Barbara Brown Taylor, "Miracle on the Beach," in her *Home by Another Way* (Boston: Cowley, 1999), 38.

God rescues people and then lays down the law. We should pause to notice that this is one part of biblical religion that offends secularists. As a matter of fact, until our own magnificent defeat, this is a part of biblical religion that offends all of us. We chafe under commandments. They nick our pride and cramp our style. We think they're for children. In a secularist frame of mind, we human beings think of obedience to God's law as a distasteful, even cowardly, knuckling under to somebody else's will.

> "When one gives up Christian belief one thereby deprives oneself of the right to Christian morality. . . . Christianity is a system, a consistently thought out and complete view of things. If one breaks out of it a fundamental idea, the belief in God, one thereby breaks the whole thing to pieces: one has nothing of any consequence left in one's hands. . . . Christian morality is a command: its origin is transcendental . . . it possesses truth only if God is truth — it stands or falls with the belief in God."
>
> Friedrich Nietzsche[5]

But when we have been shorn of such self-deception, we can see that God's law is in fact one more exhibit of God's grace. What God carved in stone at Sinai was a recipe for real freedom. I know it sounds paradoxical to say that we get freedom by obeying God's commandments, but that's actually the way things go. Sin traps people and

5. Friedrich Nietzsche, *Twilight of the Idols,* Expeditions of an Untimely Man, Section 5.

74

makes them wilt; godly obedience liberates people and helps them flourish. The Ten Commandments are guides for a free and flourishing life. They say, "Do this and you will thrive." Or else they say, "Don't do this: it'll kill you." God's commandments are all pro-life.

Maybe this isn't as strange as it sounds. Imagine what the world would be like if for even one day everybody lived in complete obedience to the Ten Commandments: for one day, no murder; no stealing; no adultery that breaks up families. Instead, for one day all would tell the truth, give to those in need, protect their neighbors from harm, honor their parents, worship God with an appetite, and thus express love to God and to neighbor in a long undertow of joy.

Needless to say, even covenant people have often ignored this recipe. In fact, while still camped out at Sinai (Exod. 32:1-6), the children of Israel persuaded Moses' brother Aaron to make them a god alongside God — a golden calf, a cud-chewing stud like the idols in Egypt. (Moses could get the Israelites out of Egypt, but it wasn't as easy to get Egypt out of the Israelites.)

In fact, the Old Testament shows us a lot of sin and other heavy weather inside the covenant of grace. The people of God display the whole range of obedience and sloth, piety and treachery. Thus, the pages of the Old Testament give us not only the wisdom of Solomon and the psalms of David; not only the faithfulness of Samuel and the patience of Job; but also a sequence of macho judges, wicked kings, false prophets, and unholy priests. King David himself — simultaneously godly and corrupt — shows us what God must deal with. God loves his people (David is "a man after God's own heart"), but God hates the sin that keeps dragging his people backward toward slavery (David nearly ruins Israel by his own adultery, deceit, and conspiracy to commit murder). So by way of the "latter prophets" (Isaiah through Malachi), God warns of coming disaster. Almost desperately, the prophets call people to return to God. But the people of God have "a stubborn and rebellious heart" that will not face facts. "No one repents of wickedness, saying, 'What have I done!'" (Jer. 8:6). In response to such stubbornness, the God of the prophets sounds weary at times, exasperated at the perversity of people who worship piously and also chisel their neighbors. Exodus, law, prophets, priests, kings — seemingly none of these can stop the shipwreck of Israel and her mission to the nations.

> "Almighty and most merciful Father, we have erred and strayed from thy ways, like lost sheep. We have followed too much the devices and desires of our own hearts. We have offended against thy holy laws. We have left undone those things which we ought to have done, and we have done those things which we ought not to have done, and there is no health in us."
>
> A General Confession, *Book of Common Prayer*

What's striking, once more, is the persistence of God's grace. God refuses to let the shipwreck happen. So the prophets tell of God's judgment, and they foretell the exile of his people. But they also see God's salvation on the horizon, and they want it with the whole force of their hearts. As we've noted before, the prophets long for a new age when God will shake his people free from their enemies, just as he had done in Egypt. In the new age God's people will respond with glad obedience, the rich helping the poor and the strong lifting the weak. As God's grace spreads across the land, the lame will begin to dance; the blind will gaze at a world they have never seen before; the deaf will hear the song of a lark. Covenant obligations and promises, broken and forgotten, will be fulfilled. In a word, the prophets long for shalom. Hearing the voice of God in their souls, they assure people that God's kingdom of peace will come one day, and that a particular figure, weighty with centuries of longing and promise, will bring it near.

Redemption

Incarnation, Atonement, Resurrection

The Old Testament prophets speak of the Messiah. They speak of a particular person who will inaugurate the new age. Sometimes they speak of the one to come as if he would be a warrior king. As David had slain the Philistines, so the Messiah, the new David, will slay God's enemies (Isa. 63:1-6). Alternatively, the one to come will be a man of sorrows, slaughtered like an animal for the sins of others (Isa. 53). He will be a victorious king or a suffering servant, or maybe both, but in any case he will be "anointed." That is, like kings and priests he will have oil poured over him as a sign that God has picked him out for special work. Or, like a prophet, the Messiah might be anointed with the very Spirit of God (Isa. 61:1; Luke 4:18).

The Hebrew word for the expected one, *Messiah,* means "the anointed one." (Greek-speaking Jews translated *Messiah* with the title *Christ.*) The Messiah would be the greatest of men, a twig growing out of the trunk of King David that would eventually dwarf David himself. Or else, as the prophets sometimes put it, the one to come would be a twig growing out of *the Lord* (Isa. 4:2). The Messiah would be called "Mighty God" or "God-with-us" (Isa. 9:6; 7:14). He would be the Lord himself suddenly coming to his temple (Mal. 3:1). In other words, the Messiah might be human or he might be divine, but in either case he would save his people.

What few imagined is that the Messiah would be *both* human and divine. Nobody foresaw explicitly that God (or, more exactly, the eternal Son of God) would come in the flesh. By the time of Jesus' birth, most of his contemporaries were looking more for a man than for God, and more for a political champion than for a suffering servant. They wanted somebody who could get Rome off their back and Caesar out of their hair. They were looking for a man who could become their king.

What they got was their King who had become a man — God incarnate, God with a thumbprint and, for all we know, seasonal hay fever. Trying to describe the novelty of the incarnation, the New Testament writers borrowed from every source they could think of. They

77

borrowed from wisdom literature and prophecy; they borrowed from history, poetry, and apocalypse. They strained to describe one who was simultaneously "the reflection of God's glory and the exact imprint of God's very being" (Heb. 1:3) and also a particular Jew, the son of Mary, a man who had not especially impressed the people he grew up with (Mark 6:1-6).

Working all their sources, the inspired writers of Scripture tell us that he is the Son of God, Son of Man, Lord, and Christ. He is word and wisdom, the second Adam, the end of the law, the light of the world. He is high priest and apostle. Fulfilling prophetic promises, he is both King of kings and the suffering servant who was obedient all the way to death on a cross. He is both the sacrificial lamb of God who takes away the sin of the world and the good shepherd who lays down his life for his sheep.

As these last examples show, Jesus' mission was to die. The shadow of the cross fell across his cradle. The only Son of God was born in Bethlehem in order to absorb the inevitable penalty of our sin. Of course, he came to do more than that — much more. The Scriptures offer multiple reasons for his coming. He came "to destroy the works of the devil" (1 John 3:8). He came "to deal with sin" and to fulfill the law (Rom. 8:3-4). He came "to seek out and to save the lost" (Luke 19:10). In his longest reach, he came "to gather up all things in himself," or "to reconcile to himself all things" (Eph. 1:10; Col. 1:20). The Scriptures use a riot of terms and images to describe the force of Jesus' work, but one way or another they all say that Jesus Christ came

> *Atonement is a self-sacrificial act or process that makes up for sin, either ours or another's, and therefore tends to reconcile the sinner with the one sinned against. Atonement leads toward "at-one-ment."*

to put right what we human beings had put wrong by our sin. Thus, he came in order to be "the atoning sacrifice for our sins" (1 John 4:10) and "to give his life a ransom for many" (Mark 10:45).

Why was atonement so necessary? The main reason is that we human beings can't atone for ourselves. Our sin is great; our power to make up for it is meager. In fact, we often refuse even to admit our sin. Like the people described in Jeremiah, we deny wrongdoing. If our sin gets exposed, we feel humiliated, and if we have to confess it, we feel mortified. So we avoid these things if we can. Trussing up our dignity with the temporary walls of self-deception, we avoid penance because we think that penance (the discipline of submitting ourselves to the due penalty for sin) is disgraceful.

Jesus Christ entered the world to offer the penance we refuse. I don't mean that he confessed his own sins, of which there weren't any. I mean that he acted like a repentant sinner. He got himself baptized, like every sinner. He absorbed accusations. He accepted rebuke without protest. He endured gossip about his choice of friends and his eating and drinking habits. Especially near the end, Jesus endured the kind of mockery that shreds a person's dignity. And then, at the end, he died slowly on an instrument that the Romans had invented to kill their enemies, and first to humiliate them. And so on Good Friday, Christians observe the death of a perfect penitent, one who stood under the misery of the world's sin, who absorbed evil without passing it on, and who therefore cut the terrible lines of lawlessness and revenge that have looped down the centuries from the time of Cain and Lamech.

That was Friday. But "the third day he rose again from the dead" in the central event of the Christian religion and of all human history. Christians who make this confession are not talking about the resurrection of faith in the disciples, or of hope in the women at the tomb, or of tulips in the spring. They are confessing the real resurrection of a horribly dead Jesus. As the Apostles' Creed says pointedly, "he was crucified, dead, *buried*."

But on the third day, in a spectacular miracle, Jesus Christ rose from the dead and changed the history of the world. The first message of the gospel, a message with power to straighten the spine of every believer, is simply this: "The Lord is risen." "He is risen indeed!" Preaching, sacraments, evangelism, Christian social action — even worship on Sunday instead of on Saturday — all center on the resurrection of Jesus Christ. To the desperate and bewildered, Christians say, "The Lord is risen." To doubters, Christians say, "The Lord is risen." To martyrs who sing to God while their enemies set them on fire, Christians say, "The Lord is risen." To poor people in Bangladesh, or Honduras, or Turkey, who suffer first the indignity of their poverty and then the desolation of being blown out of their houses by hurricanes or washed out by flood — all because they are too poor to build anything on habitable land — to these people Christians say, "The Lord is risen."

Proclamation of the resurrection of Jesus isn't nearly everything Christians have to offer the world, but it's the platform for everything they have to offer. Every Christian hospital, college, orphanage, media ministry, counseling service, political party, relief agency, and AIDS clinic builds on this platform. Christian *hope* builds on this platform. In fact, a Christian's hope rises with Christ because Christians see in his resurrection that God's grace cannot be defeated, not even by death itself.

> "How fair and lovely is the hope which the Lord gave to the dead when He lay down like them beside them. Rise up and come forth and sing praise to Him who has raised you from destruction."
>
> Syrian Orthodox Liturgy

What *was* it that even death could not defeat? I just said it was God's grace, but I might as well have said it was the kingdom of God.

I'll say much more about the kingdom of God in the next chapter, but for now we should note simply this: Jesus' resurrection validated his role as the one who brought the kingdom near. In fact, Jesus' preaching, his model prayer, his miracles, his choice of friends, and the whole tenor of his life brought God and the kingdom of God much nearer than people wanted. Jesus brought the kingdom too close for comfort, and this is one of the reasons people wanted him dead. So when Jesus taught his disciples that "those who want to save their life will lose it, and those who lose their life for my sake will find it" (Matt. 16:25), he not only summarized his ministry but also anticipated its climax: his own death and resurrection.

Dying and Rising in Union with Christ

But how might a person *get in on* the powerful work of Jesus Christ? According to Scripture, the death and resurrection of Christ are "for us," "for many," "for all" (Rom. 5:8, 15, 18). He was slain "for our trespasses and was raised for our justification" (4:25). But, again, how would a person receive these benefits? After all, according to popular thinking, Jesus Christ is either in history or in heaven; he's either "back there" or else "up there." In either case, he's somewhere else. The problem, Calvin wrote, is that "as long as Christ remains outside of us . . . all that he has suffered and done for the salvation of the human race remains useless . . . ; all that he possesses is nothing to us until we grow into one body with him."[6]

"Until we grow into one body with him." Calvin is talking about union with Christ, and, in the same breath, about the Christian church. What Calvin knew is that Jesus Christ did not rise alone. He rose as the head of a whole body of people elected to have faith in him, to benefit from him, and to extend his mission in the world. Believers unite with Christ through "the secret energy of the Holy Spirit" and through faith (itself God's gift), and believers express this faith and

6. Calvin, *Institutes,* 1:537 (3.1.1).

absorb this energy through wholehearted participation in the church and her means of grace. The church, says Calvin, is "our mother" who "nourishes us at her breast."[7]

In New Testament thinking, nobody gains union with Christ by himself. Of course, believers may enjoy personal, even mystical, communion with Christ in prayer and meditation. (I have Jesuit friends who begin each day with "the Jesus prayer," repeatedly saying, "O Lord Jesus Christ, Son of God, have mercy on me," till they sense that the Lord himself has come to reassure them of his mercy.) It is possible — in fact, normal — to share with Jesus Christ the day's events, joys, and sorrows, even the slight ones, and to do so not just by deliberate prayer, but also by perceiving his presence with us in these events and emotions.

> *"Those who have not learned to ask God for childish things will have less readiness to ask Him for great ones. We must not be too high-minded. I fancy we may sometimes be deterred from small prayers by a sense of our own dignity rather than of God's."*
>
> C. S. Lewis[8]

But even in private acts of communion, customized to fit our personal circumstances, we are never just free agents. We are members of a worldwide and local body, a whole team of believers, a "cloud of witnesses" (Heb. 12:1). In his commentary on the Heidelberg Catechism, Zacharius Ursinus says that "when anyone prays alone in his closet,

7. Calvin, *Institutes,* 2:1016 (4.1.4).

8. C. S. Lewis, *Letters to Malcolm: Chiefly on Prayer* (New York: Harcourt Brace, 1964), 23.

the whole church prays with him in affection and desire."[9] And so, appropriately, the classic events by which a person attaches to Christ are corporate. The preaching of the gospel is a corporate event. Baptism and the Lord's Supper are *church* sacraments, intended to bind to Christ and to each other a whole body of people who don't necessarily even like each other very much. Some are originally Jews, some Greeks. Some lean left in their politics, some right. Some want traditional church music, some contemporary. Like spokes, the only place these folks fit together is at their hub. Somehow they must all fit "into" Christ.

How would this work?

Think again of the people of Israel spilling out of slavery in Egypt and headed for the promised land. To get there they had to pass through a near-death experience at the Red Sea (Exod. 14). In a striking expression, St. Paul says that the children of Israel were "baptized into Moses" in the Red Sea (1 Cor. 10:2), just as New Testament people are baptized into Jesus Christ.

What could this peculiar language possibly mean?

Paul is talking about an event that changes a person's very identity. Before the Red Sea, an Israelite was a slave to a foreign power. After the Red Sea, an Israelite was a liberated child of God, belonging to the people whom God was leading forward into a whole new history of fellowship and promise. Centuries later, Jews would celebrate Passover as if they had the Exodus in their own memory bank. Even today, "I am an orthodox Jew" means "I am a slave, whom God led out of Egypt by the hand of Moses, and to whom God gave the law at Sinai. I am a Moses-Exodus-Sinai person, a member of the people who were forever changed by this man and these events."[10]

The Israelites were baptized into Moses in the main events of the covenant of grace in its Old Testament phase. Christians get baptized

---

9. Ursinus, *The Commentary of Dr. Zacharius Ursinus on the Heidelberg Catechism*, trans. G. W. Williard (Grand Rapids: Eerdmans, 1954), 628.

10. See Lewis B. Smedes, *All Things Made New* (Grand Rapids: Eerdmans, 1970), 143-44.

into the death and resurrection of Jesus Christ, the main events of the covenant of grace in its New Testament phase. In this new era, membership in the covenant of grace is marked not by circumcision of males, but by baptism of faithful males and females, Jews and Greeks, slaves and free persons — and, we might add, American Baptists and Syrian Orthodox. They were all "raised with Christ" when he was raised on the third day, the pioneer of a new humanity. (In Romans 5 Paul calls Jesus the "second Adam.") Jesus' resurrection, the "second Exodus," says once more that God has set his people free.

But to profit from this event, people need to get *into* it. So in the sacrament of baptism the followers of Christ deliberately reenact his dying and rising, and most include infants in this reenactment, believing that they too belong to the covenant of grace. A baptized person gets immersed in water or sprinkled with water (my own opinion is that sprinkling is only an appetizer) in a near-death experience that publicly marks her as belonging to Jesus Christ. She is "lowered into death" and is then "raised to life" in an identity-forming event that says to the world, "This is a person who belongs to Calvary, to Easter, to Christ." Her confession is not "I am a person formed by Exodus and Sinai," but "I am a person formed by the cross and the resurrection." These are my events because I belong to the Lord of these events. And I belong to the *people* formed by these events. Because I have died and risen with Jesus Christ, I live with the people of Christ, under the shadow of Christ, in a world that has been changed by Christ and that will one day be wholly transformed by Christ.[11]

Through baptism God identifies a person as being "in Christ." Through faith the baptized person identifies *herself* in the same way. (She does this later if she is an infant or on the spot if she is an adult.) Her profession of faith says, "I am a person of the cross and resurrection of Jesus Christ, and of all that they mean." She might even sign her letters "in Christ," and, as we can see, she might mean a great deal by those two words.

The gospel says that a baptized person enters a new world, a

11. Smedes, *All Things Made New*, 145-46.

> Q. What do you believe
>   concerning "the holy catholic church"?
> A. I believe that the Son of God,
>   through his Spirit and Word,
>   out of the entire human race,
>   from the beginning of the world to its end,
>   gathers, protects, and preserves for himself
>   a community chosen for eternal life
>   and united in true faith.
>   And of this community I am and always will be
>   a living member.
>
> The Heidelberg Catechism,
Question and Answer 54

"promised land" where people may enjoy "the glorious liberty of the children of God" (Rom. 8:21, RSV). Everybody wants liberty. The problem is that everybody wants it on his own terms. But salvation doesn't work that way. God doesn't save people (from slavery, from addiction, from sin and shame) and then cut them loose to do what they want, because without the guidance of God "doing what we want" is a recipe for falling right back into slavery.

So, to prevent a relapse, God preserves those who die and rise with Christ in baptism and who respond to their baptism with faith (or to their faith with baptism). How? The Spirit of God empowers believers to "keep the rhythm going" where dying and rising are concerned.[12] Yielding to the Spirit of God, a believer seeks the death of her old self and the resurrection of her new self. That is, she puts her arrogance to death and raises her humility to life. She puts envy to death and raises

---

12. See especially Rom. 6:1-14 and Col. 3:1-17.

> *"Now we shall possess a right definition of faith if we call it a firm and certain knowledge of God's benevolence toward us, founded upon the truth of the freely given promise in Christ, both revealed to our minds and sealed upon our hearts through the Holy Spirit."*
>
> John Calvin, *Institutes of the Christian Religion*[13]

gratitude to life. She puts rage to death and raises gentleness to life. When she breaks this good rhythm for a time, she confesses her sins, which is another form of dying because it kills us to admit we are in the wrong. What's wonderful is that when a person goes through the "little death" of confession to imitate Jesus' big death at Golgotha, she also rises toward new life, like Jesus walking out of his tomb. Confession of sin is an enormously *freeing* thing to do.

Once reformed, a Christian life needs continual reformation. Even our reforms need reforming, and especially when we grow proud of them or despairing of them. And the central rhythm of reform is dying and rising with Christ, practiced over and over till it becomes a way of being.

Take compassion as an example of dying and rising. A compassionate Christian feels distress at another's suffering and wants to relieve it. His willingness to "weep with those who weep" (Rom. 12:15) represents the death of scorn ("He made his own bed; let him lie in it") and the death of aloofness ("Why should I care about people tortured by a military dictator in some country I can't even pronounce?"). Compassion represents the death of our old self, with its emotional stinginess, and the birth of our new self, with its emotional generos-

13. Calvin, *Institutes of the Christian Religion*, 1:551 (3.2.7).

> *"It is amusing to see souls who, while they are at prayer, fancy they are willing to be despised and publicly insulted for the love of God, yet afterwards do all they can to hide their small defects; if anyone unjustly accuses them of a fault, God deliver us from their outcries!"*
>
> Teresa of Ávila[14]

ity. The compassionate person unites with Jesus Christ in "losing his life to find it" by getting out of his shell and into the full range of the world's joys and sorrows.

Meanwhile, the recipient of compassion gains vitality too. Love vivifies us. The sorrow and tears of a compassionate friend say to us, beyond words, that we matter to him — and to *God,* who expresses his love incarnately through family members, teachers, good friends, and even kind-hearted strangers. If the givers and receivers of compassion are believers, they will connect their exchange to the suffering love of the Son of God, who did not remain aloof, but made himself vulnerable "for us and for our salvation."

The "Double Grace" and the Virtues of Christ

Dying and rising with Christ cannot become our life's rhythm without supernatural regeneration by the Holy Spirit. The person who belongs to Jesus Christ in the fullest sense must be regenerated, or "born again," in a supernatural act of God, which is the first event in a

14. St. Teresa of Ávila, from *The Interior Castle,* trans. E. A. Peers (New York: Sheed and Ward, 1946), quoted in *Ordinary Graces: Christian Teachings on the Interior Life,* ed. Lorraine Kisly with an intro. by Philip Zalieski (New York: Bell Tower, 2000), 38.

lifelong conversion of a person from her old self to her new self. This lifelong conversion is called sanctification (or "becoming holier"), and regeneration is the explosion that starts its motor. God alone regenerates, but we answer God's calling to become sanctified people by trying to starve our old self (the one that is envious and hardhearted) and to feed our new self (the one that is grateful and compassionate) in the rhythm that I described earlier.

If we think of the terrible, deadening effects of sin, then the regeneration of a person's love for God and for neighbors really is a kind of miracle. In the terms Jesus used to describe the prodigal son, regeneration is the mysterious turn of his heart toward home "when he came to himself" (Luke 15:17).

> "This is regeneration. . . . [I]t is an entirely supernatural work, one that is at the same time most powerful and most pleasing, a marvelous, hidden, and inexpressible work, which is not lesser than or inferior in power to that of creation or of raising the dead."
>
> The Canons of Dort, third/fourth points, article 12

But God not only regenerates and sanctifies; God also forgives and reconciles[15] by a sheer act of grace. The name for God's act of forgiving sinners and reconciling them to himself is justification. In a word, justification is God's *acceptance* of sinners, on account of the atoning work of Jesus Christ. Justification is a name for the divine act that makes us "right with God." Like the waiting father in the parable of the prodigal son, God welcomes us back from our jour-

---

15. It's hard to know the logical and temporal order of these acts, and we won't take time to join the old theological discussion of them.

ney into disgrace, forgiving our sins and, as in Eden, clothing our shame with his own love. To understand God's acceptance with our heart as well as our mind, what we need is the sense of exultation in the parable:

> While he was still far off, his father saw him and was filled with compassion; he ran and put his arms around him and kissed him. Then the son said to him, "Father, I have sinned against heaven and before you; I am no longer worthy to be called your son." But the father said to his slaves, "Quickly, bring out a robe — the best one — and put it on him; put a ring on his finger and sandals on his feet. And get the fatted calf and kill it, and let us eat and celebrate; for this son of mine was dead and is alive again; he was lost and is found!" (Luke 15:20-24)

Q. How are you right with God?
A. Only by true faith in Jesus Christ.
   Even though my conscience accuses me . . .
   and even though I am still inclined toward all evil,
   nevertheless,
        without my deserving it at all,
        out of sheer grace,
   God grants and credits to me
   the perfect satisfaction, righteousness, and holiness
        of Christ,
        as if I had never sinned.

                              The Heidelberg Catechism,
                              Question and Answer 60

Calvin called sanctification and justification "a double grace" and thought of this double grace as the principal benefit of uniting with Jesus Christ through faith.[16] I know that such terms as *regeneration, justification,* and *sanctification* can weigh a bit heavy on us. But they are part of the vocabulary of every educated Christian, and each refers to a real event with real effects. As Calvin says repeatedly, the double grace releases us, relieves us, redeems us. Since salvation is by grace alone, we are free from slavery to sin, free from slavery to self-help schemes, free from slavery to the opinions of others. We are free to lean on God with all our weight, giving ourselves over to a prayerful and joyful life marked by a quiet conscience and fullness of faith. After all, the basic things wrong with us — guilt and corruption — have already been addressed by God through the double grace. God removes our guilt by justifying or "rectifying" us and removes our corruption by the long-term process of sanctification. Some Christians in the Wesleyan tradition go a step further, believing in "entire sanctification." So, for example, the Statement of Faith of Asbury College describes entire sanctification as

> that act of divine grace, through the baptism with the Holy Spirit, by which the heart is cleansed from all sin and filled with the pure love of God. This is a definite, instantaneous work of grace, subsequent to regeneration, wrought in the heart of a believer, resulting from full consecration and faith in the cleansing merit of the blood of Jesus Christ.

Many of us Christians emphasize sanctification because we know the depth and width of human corruption and how miserably hard it is to fix. Anybody who has tried to lose a bad habit, let alone a full-blooded addiction, knows that good intentions and a few New Year's resolutions seldom do the trick. Similarly, to break the power of sin, a Christian person needs far more than good feelings and songs about Jesus. A person needs much more than a dramatic testi-

16. Calvin, *Institutes,* 1:725 (3.11.1).

mony. A person needs to *attach* to Christ by prayer, sacraments, and listening to the Word of God. A person needs to trust Christ, to lean on him, to surrender to him, to shape his life to fit inside Christ's kingdom.

> *"The theatrics of conversion prevents true conversion. A terrible thing. Simplicity, my Jesus, give me simplicity!"*
>
> Miguel de Unamuno[17]

All this is the project not only of the Holy Spirit, who "cuts to the heart" and puts Pentecost there, but also of believers who respond by asking, "What should we *do?*" (Acts 2:37). A Christian life needs a Holy Ghost miracle, but also our own hard work. The reforming of our lives is both God's grace and our calling. "Work out your own salvation with fear and trembling," as Paul says in Philippians, "for it is God who is at work in you, enabling you both to will and to work for his good pleasure" (2:12-13). Of course this sounds paradoxical, but it also fits with Christian experience. Nobody makes any headway in a Christian life without surrender to the grace of God. And nobody makes any headway without also striving to obey God's gracious directions for covenant life. These include not only the famous Ten Commandments of the Old Testament, but also a range of glad instructions for people who would follow Jesus:

- "Let your light shine" (Matt. 5:16);
- "Hate what is evil; hold fast to what is good" (Rom. 12:9);

17. Miguel de Unamuno, *The Private World: Selections from the Diario Íntimo and Selected Letters, 1890-1936,* trans. Anthony Kerrigan, Allen Lacy, and Martin Nozick, Bollingen series 85, vol. 2 (Princeton: Princeton University, 1984), 42.

- "Whatever is true, whatever is honorable . . . ; if there is any excellence . . . think about these things" (Phil. 4:8);
- "Pursue righteousness" (1 Tim. 6:11);
- "Remind them . . . to be gentle" (Tit. 3:1-2);
- "Bear with one another" (Eph. 4:2);
- "Clothe yourselves with love" (Col. 3:14);
- "Be imitators of God" (Eph. 5:1);
- "Strive first for the kingdom of God" (Matt. 6:33);
- "Bear one another's burdens and so fulfill the law of Christ" (Gal. 6:2, RSV).

By opening his heart to the grace of God and by striving to obey God's will, a Christian may acquire the virtues that fit a Christian life and may begin to perform the good works that flow from them. It's not that good works save anybody. It's just that they *demonstrate* God's saving grace in a person's life. We are not saved by good works, but neither are we saved without them.

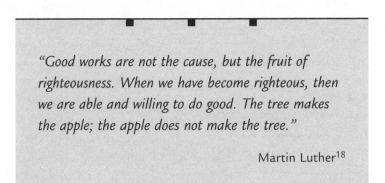

"*Good works are not the cause, but the fruit of righteousness. When we have become righteous, then we are able and willing to do good. The tree makes the apple; the apple does not make the tree.*"

Martin Luther[18]

In a key passage, Paul refers to the qualities of a Christian's life as if they were garments: "Clothe yourselves with compassion, kindness, humility, meekness, and patience. Bear with one another and, if any-

18. Martin Luther, *A Commentary on Galatians,* ed. and abr. by Theodore Graebner (Grand Rapids: Zondervan, 1939), 89.

one has a complaint against another, forgive each other" (Col. 3:12-13). C. S. Lewis reminds us that a child likes to go to a clothes box full of grownup outfits. The child wears a coat that's too big and a hat that falls down over her eyes. She clumps around in grownup shoes and she clips on earrings that swing down to the middle of her neck. It's all a kind of pretending, but it's also a kind of preparing, because every child wants one day to be a person who fits into clothes of this size.[19]

Christians are people who dress up like Christ, not because we want to deceive people into thinking we are better than we are, but because the only way we can *become* better than we are is by trying on our grownup clothes.

Why try on these virtues? Because they please God by restoring shalom. Because they express the image of God. The reason they do these things is that the virtues Paul recommends are *Christ's* virtues. To put on these virtues is to put on *Christ* (Rom. 13:14). To weep with those who weep, to accept the role of a servant, to give up anger when we have a right to be angry — to do these things is to acquire the character of a person who fits in with Jesus Christ. Christian virtues make up the family uniform of the followers of Christ. They are the baptismal robe of those who have been raised with Christ.

And so a Christian experiences revival not only when God tastes sweeter to her but also when she controls her sharp tongue. She reforms not only by losing herself in exultant worship but also by keeping in touch with family members she would rather ignore. She prays to God when she doesn't feel like it, listens to boring people at least for a while, drives her car patiently among impatient drivers. She develops a heart for the lost and wants to help win them for Jesus Christ. Always she longs to grow in her knowledge of Christ. She doesn't think of her witness to the grace of God as something that is always above and beyond her daily work. She is ready to give account of her hope in Christ, but she does this with her work as well as with her words. In fact, she attempts to live her whole life in a way that extends the reach of Jesus Christ.

19. Lewis, *Mere Christianity,* 161.

> *"Passing affections easily produce words; and words are cheap; . . . Christian practice is a costly laborious thing. The self-denial that is required of Christians, and the narrowness of the way that leads to life, don't consist in words, but in practice. Hypocrites may much more easily be brought to talk like saints, than to act like saints."*
>
> Jonathan Edwards[20]

Reforming All Things

Meanwhile, in the fellowship of the Christian community, the redeemed person embarks on a life's adventure — to discover the purposes of God and to make them her own; to discover the ways of the kingdom and to follow in those ways; to uncover the "mind of Christ" and to strive to become like-minded. Because the mind of Christ includes looking not only to one's own interests, but also to the interests of others (Phil. 2:4-5), she prays and works for people who need the grace of Jesus Christ in some obvious way:

> The flunk-outs and drop-outs and burned-outs. The broke and the broken. The drug heads and the divorced. The HIV-positive and the herpes-ridden. The brain-damaged, the incurably ill. The barren and the pregnant too many times or at the wrong time. The overemployed, the underemployed, the unemployed. The unemployable. The swindled, the shoved aside, the replaced. The parents with children living on the streets. . . . The

20. Jonathan Edwards, *Religious Affections* (1746), ed. John E. Smith (New Haven: Yale University Press, 1959), 411.

lonely, the incompetent, the stupid. The emotionally starved or the emotionally dead.[21]

Faith in Jesus Christ includes faith in his program. The faithful person practices self-giving love and trusts that he won't be a fool to do it. He practices humility and trusts that humility is actually a sign of strength. He takes on "the form of a servant" and trusts that this is the kind of life God will vindicate because servanthood is part of the life of heaven. A person who is in good spiritual shape might even undertake his service with a certain joy. As the Heidelberg Catechism puts it, in "the coming-to-life of the new self" we have "wholehearted joy in God through Christ and a delight to do every kind of good as God wants us to" (Question and Answer 90). "Every kind of good" points to the wide scope of God's program of redemption, including the reconciliation of "all things, whether on earth or in heaven" (Col. 1:20).

Thinking along these lines, Abraham Kuyper told a story at Princeton Theological Seminary when he gave his Stone Lectures there in 1898. A sixteenth-century plague had ruined the Italian city of Milan, and Cardinal Borromeo had bravely stayed to feed and to pray for those who were dying. Kuyper admired Cardinal Borromeo's piety, but he admired John Calvin's even more:

> During the plague, which in the 16th century tormented Geneva, Calvin acted better and more wisely, for he not only cared incessantly for the spiritual needs of the sick, but at the same time introduced hitherto unsurpassed hygienic measures whereby the ravages of the plague were arrested.[22]

At their best, Reformed Christians take a very big view of redemption because they take a very big view of fallenness. If all has been created good and all has been corrupted, then all must be redeemed. God

21. Dallas Willard, *The Divine Conspiracy,* 123-24.
22. Kuyper, *Calvinism: Six Stone Foundation Lectures* (Grand Rapids: Eerdmans, 1943), 120.

isn't content to save souls; God wants to save bodies too. God isn't content to save human beings in their individual activities; God wants to save social systems and economic structures too. If the management/labor structure contains built-in antagonism, then it needs to be redeemed. If the health care delivery system reaches only the well-to-do, then it needs to be reformed. The same goes for hostile relationships of race, gender, or class. The same goes for proud and scornful attitudes among heterosexuals toward homosexuals. Landlord and tenant, student and teacher, husband and wife — these and countless other roles and relationships may develop warped expectations and unfair practices. The same goes for certain forms of popular entertainment, with their tendency to violate taboos in order to gain an edge, draw a crowd, and make a buck.

Everything corrupt needs to be redeemed, and that includes the whole natural world, which both sings and groans. The whole natural world, in all its glory and pain, needs the redemption that will bring shalom. The world isn't divided into a sacred realm and a secular realm, with redemptive activity confined to the sacred zone. The whole world belongs to God, the whole world has fallen, and so the whole world needs to be redeemed — every last person, place, organization, and program; all "rocks and trees and skies and seas"; in fact, "every square inch," as Abraham Kuyper said. The whole creation is "a theater for the mighty works of God," first in creation and then in re-creation.[23]

English Puritans understood this idea very well. John Calvin pointed the way, but it was the Puritans who got really fired up about the need for redemption in every place and structure where sin had left its mark. We sometimes think of Puritans as people with small obsessions centering on worldly amusements. But they had bigger fields to till. Thus, the Puritan minister Thomas Case preached to the English House of Commons in 1641:

> Reformation must be universal . . . reform all places, all persons
> and callings; reform the benches of judgment . . . reform the

23. Kuyper, *Calvinism*, 162.

universities, reform the cities, reform the countries . . . reform the Sabbath, reform the ordinances, the worship of God . . . you have more work to do than I can speak. . . . Every plant which my heavenly father hath not planted shall be rooted up.[24]

You can see, adds Nicholas Wolterstorff, why a seventeenth-century English writer could say, "I had rather see coming toward me a whole regiment with drawn swords, than one lone Calvinist convinced that he is doing the will of God."[25]

But where will our lone Calvinist (or other Christian) find the will of God? How does she know what needs reforming? What standard may she use to tell what's corrupt? If her city has a crumbling economy and city officials propose to shore it up by legalizing and taxing casino gambling, will the Christian reformer swing into action? If so, by what authority? And what, exactly, will she do? Pray on her knees? Write a letter to the editor of the local paper? Organize a referendum that would prohibit local gambling? Wait till the casino opens and hand out tracts to its customers? Hack into the casino's computers and mess them up?

Here we can see why Puritans and others wanted reform *according to the Word of God.* They wanted a straightedge to guide their reforms, especially because sin has twisted our thinking. They wanted an *outside* word, an inspired and infallible word, which would define "good" and "evil," not by human opinions, but by the wisdom of God. They wanted a picture of shalom and of the kingdom of God so they could see how life is supposed to go and then judge how life needs to be reformed in order to go that way. Moreover, they wanted the same Holy Spirit who had originally inspired Scripture to inspire *them* when they took Scripture in hand to read or preach it. They wanted what Calvin called "the internal testimony of the Holy Spirit" to bring the words of Scripture home to them, to validate and apply these words. That's

---

24. Quoted in Michael Walzer, *The Revolution of the Saints: A Study in the Origins of Radical Politics* (Cambridge: Harvard University Press, 1965), 1-2.

25. Wolterstorff, *Justice and Peace,* 9.

why many Christians have traditionally had a "prayer for illumination" before reading and preaching Scripture in church. They know that unless the Holy Spirit breathes through Scripture all over again as it's read, we might not hear it the right way and we might not believe it.

But in thinking about applying Scripture to life, the reformers faced a problem — namely, that it's hard to guide a program of reform by reference to the whole Bible, which is very large, or by reference to a single verse from it, which is very small. To solve this problem, Luther, Calvin, and other reformers reached for a solution at least as old as the earliest forms of the Apostles' Creed. They wrote medium-length catechisms and confessions of faith that summarized scriptural teaching in a form handy enough to be learned, or even memorized, by believers. Expectably, these documents describe God, Christ, and the Spirit; they describe the Trinity, the incarnation, and Jesus' atonement for sin. They also describe the drama of the kingdom of God, including creation, fall, and redemption.

What's striking about their teaching on redemption is that it often includes a kind of owner's manual for reforming human life. So the Heidelberg Catechism of 1563 presents the Ten Commandments to show not only where we have gone off the road but also how to get back on it. Using the rest of Scripture to fill out the meaning of the Commandments, the Catechism broadens, deepens, positivizes, and applies them. The Catechism broadens "Honor your father and mother," for example, to include honoring "all those in authority over me." It deepens "Do not murder" to forbid the "the root of murder: envy, hatred, anger, vindictiveness." Meanwhile, "do not bear false witness" turns into a positive requirement to "do what I can to guard and advance my neighbor's good name." "Do not steal" turns out to forbid "fraudulent merchandising." When preachers use the Catechism to guide their sermons, or when they teach it to their congregations, they say, in effect, that the new life in Jesus Christ has as much to do with how I buy and sell as it does with how often I pray.

Of course, such interpretations of the Commandments do not end moral discussion among Christians. They don't tell us exactly what to do about the spread of casinos, for example. They don't tell us whether tattoos are a good idea, or which styles of music best carry the message of the gospel. I suppose we could say that such interpretations of the Commandments do not end moral discussions; they start them.

Suppose I'm ready to reject "fraudulent merchandising," for example, just as the Heidelberg Catechism directs. I still have to know what *counts* as fraudulent advertising. Is it fraudulent for advertisers to sell us products by using the endorsement of celebrities who know and care little about what they endorse? Is it fraudulent for advertisers to sell us products by way of ads that titillate rather than inform? Is it fraudulent (or even lethal) for advertisers to portray as normal a pencil-thin female body profile — one that is unattainable by 95 percent of the population because those flawless ad photos are computer-assembled composites?

Scripture and the confessions give us solid principles and directions for reforming life, but they also invite us to find creative ways of applying them in the contemporary world. This is one of the reasons why a Christian college education is such an adventure for believers in Christ. In a community of faith, blessed with an abundance of intelligence, devotion, and experience, bound together by mutual respect and accountability, Christians can explore "the heights and depths" of (among other things) the contemporary world. Together, faculty, students, and staff can explore the world and its cultures before pretending to understand them; to understand them before presuming to appraise them; and to appraise them with an educated judgment gained from communion with Jesus Christ, "in whom are hidden all the treasures of wisdom" (Col. 2:3).

As we've noted before, good and evil seldom appear alone, and a Christian response to them is therefore bound to be mixed. Part of the goal of Christian higher education, then, is to "test the spirits," including all the spirits that are in competition with the Holy Spirit.[26]

26. Robert C. Roberts, *The Strengths of a Christian* (Philadelphia: Westminster, 1984), 19.

Christians want to *discern* the spirit of our own age, for example, and not just absorb it. We want to discern the offerings of contemporary culture and not just consume them.

Discernment is a feature of wisdom, which is a main goal of Christian higher education. But Christians don't seek wisdom just because it's satisfying to know how life works. Christians seek wisdom because it helps us find and follow our vocation within the kingdom of God, which has "come near" but has not yet "come home."

Vocation in the Kingdom of God

The LORD is king!

Psalm 93:1

Hate evil and love good.

Amos 5:15

Our Father in heaven. . . .
Your kingdom come.
Your will be done, on earth as it is in heaven.

Matthew 6:9-10

Strive first for the kingdom of God and his righteousness.

Matthew 6:33

The kingdom of God has come near; repent, and believe in
the good news.

Mark 1:15

Do not be conformed to this world, but be transformed by the renewing of your minds, so that you may discern what is the will of God — what is good and acceptable and perfect.

Romans 12:2

On his robe and on his thigh he has a name inscribed, "King of kings and Lord of lords."

Revelation 19:16

When the writers of psalms want redemption, they usually want it with a passion. They crave God's cleansing pardon, as Psalm 51 shows us: "Have mercy on me, O God" (v. 1). Psalmists want spiritual health, and they want it urgently: "Create in me a clean heart, O God. . . . Restore to me the joy of your salvation" (vv. 10, 12). In fact, they want God himself: "O God, . . . I seek you, my soul thirsts for you, . . . as in a dry and weary land" (Ps. 63:1).

When the scriptural people of God seek redemption, they want personal salvation, and they express their desire in what sounds like a cry of the heart. But to them redemption goes far beyond personal salvation. When biblical people want God to redeem, what they want is freedom and righteousness throughout the land. They want God to unseat Pharaoh or Caesar. They want God to drive the Midianites back across the border. They're Exodus people, after all. They're Passover people. They have a history of being squeezed by Egypt, Babylon, or Rome. In their eyes, God's redemption means justice is coming, liberation is coming, the King of all the earth is coming!

Contemporary Christians have learned this biblical language and hope. They, too, want a clean heart and a right spirit toward God. They, too, want justice to "roll down like waters, and righteousness like an everflowing stream" (Amos 5:24). (So in a praise song by Scott Underwood, "Righteousness, righteousness is what I long for.") But, following the habit of Jesus, especially in his model prayer and in his parables, perhaps contemporary Christians most often speak of their longing for the kingdom of God. It's the kingdom of God that is "the treasure in the field," or "the pearl of great price" (Matt. 13:44-46), and we can understand why. The coming of the kingdom of God represents a final state of cosmic redemption, in which God and God's creatures dwell together in harmony, righteousness, and delight. In fact, "the coming of the kingdom of God" is just the New Testament way of spelling shalom.

But now a question: Do contemporary Christians bring the same passion to their hope of redemption as people in the Bible did?

Much depends on which Christians we're talking about. Most respectable Christians do have the biblical habit of praying for the kingdom to come, but when their lives are good their prayers for the kingdom sometimes fade. People whisper their prayers for the kingdom, so that God can't quite hear them. "Your kingdom come," Christians pray, and hope it won't. "Your kingdom come," they say, "but not right away."[1] When our earthly kingdoms have had a good year, we don't necessarily long for the kingdom of God to break in. We like our own setup just fine.

God's kingdom has always sounded like good news for people whose lives are bad news. If you are a slave in a Pharaoh's kingdom, or in a Mississippi cotton kingdom, you want the kingdom of God, and you might even sing your longing in "spirituals." If you live in an African village that has been decimated by the AIDS epidemic, you want the kingdom to come so much you can think of little else. If you are a Christian woman there who lacks the cultural clout to say "No!" to men who don't care whether they kill you by having sex with you, then you want God's kingdom with every fiber of your being.

"Your kingdom come." I should explain that Christians who pray in this way are not asking for the kingdom to come into *existence*. God's kingdom has been in existence forever. It was present at creation when God the king said, "Let us create," and then made the plant and animal kingdoms to fit inside his own. God's kingdom was present in paradise when our first parents turned against it. Since then people have regularly revolted against God's sovereignty, or ignored it. That's why Jesus taught his disciples to pray for a miracle: that people would stop rebelling against God's will and stop ignoring it and would start trying instead to conform their will to God's. In the Lord's Prayer, "Your kingdom come" *means* "Your will be done on earth, as it is in heaven." And, for that to happen, hearts will have to be regenerated, and much more besides.

1. Justo L. González, ¡*Alabadle!* (Nashville: Abingdon, 1996), 18.

Kingdoms inside Kingdoms

The kingdom of God is the sphere of God's sovereignty — namely, the whole universe. In the vivid imagery of Isaiah 66:1, heaven is God's "throne" and the earth is God's "footstool." God is *God,* after all, the author of galaxies, the redeemer of all the earth, the "King of kings and Lord of lords."

To this last statement Christians sing the Hallelujah Chorus, but they don't always reflect on what logically follows. To say that God (or Christ) is "King of kings" implies that God is the supreme ruler, but not the only one. Below God, there are also presidents, prime ministers, chairmen, chiefs, and shahs. In fact, to some extent we are all rulers just because God has created us in his own image to have "responsible dominion." What follows is that we all have a little kingdom. That is, we all have a certain range in which our will is effective. We all have a particular sphere over which we "have our say."[2] When we are babies, we have baby kingdoms. Our will has a short range, but high effectiveness, as when we determine whether anybody else in the house will get a night's sleep. When we are college students we have bigger kingdoms, including, for instance, a job and half a dorm room. We also have a say over the depth of our education, given how much of it depends on our own effort and reflection. By the time we get to be middle managers, heads of households, self-employed professionals, or agency chiefs, our kingdom expands further. The same is true the first time we buy a piece of real property, and especially a house. "A person's house is his castle" because it's a proper place for a person to reign.

But none of us reigns in isolation. Much of the time we have our say only in community with others. This is true, for example, when we vote or accept membership on a council. Usually we have to fit our kingdoms inside somebody else's bigger kingdom. (Middle managers report to upper managers, and college presidents report to college boards.) But even with such accountability, we still exercise appropri-

2. Dallas Willard, *Conspiracy,* 20.

ate control of our coming and going, our choice of associates, our intimacies, and much else. In fact, having our say in these matters is so valuable that losing it amounts to a kind of disaster. That's why it's so humiliating to be jailed or enslaved.[3] That's why it's so devastating to be raped, or bulldozed out of your house. People in these circumstances lose a big part of their kingdom. They feel as if they've been deposed.

What we must see, now, is that successful living in God's world depends not only on taking responsibility for our own realm and preserving it if we can. Success also depends on meshing our kingdom with the kingdoms of others — learning to share living space, for example, or to take part in good teamwork. Successful living depends especially on fitting our small kingdom inside God's big kingdom, always recalling where we got our dominion in the first place. Each of us is king or queen over a little. God's kingdom is "over all," as the psalmists liked to say.[4]

I said in the last chapter that Jesus' career witnessed to the kingdom of God and that Jesus' resurrection vindicated his dominion. In Jesus Christ, God's kingly reign showed through much more clearly for a time. Jesus' exorcisms demonstrated God's authority over demons that stir in us. Jesus' healings showed God's power over diseases that sicken us. Jesus' nature miracles — walking on water, making lots of wine for a wedding celebration — previewed the wonders of the age to come.

We now live in between Jesus' first and second advents. During his first coming, Jesus brought God's kingdom near (Mark 1:15), but Jesus also pointed toward the fullness of the kingdom still to come. In fact, as we've just seen, he taught his disciples to pray for it: "Our Father in heaven, . . . your kingdom come" (Matt. 6:9-10). Christians today still make this prayer to God because we have had the incarnation of Jesus but not his return "with power and great glory" (Luke 21:27). In his earthly career Jesus changed the world, but he didn't perfect it.

3. Willard, *Conspiracy*, 21.
4. Willard, *Conspiracy*, 23.

He healed many sick people, but not everybody. He cast out some demons, but not all. So far as we know, he turned water into wine only at Cana. He invited just one disciple to walk on water, and with mixed results.

So in his first advent Jesus did much, but he also left much to do. Remarkably, he left much for his followers to do. He told them to ask, seek, and knock (Matt. 7:7); to "strive first for the kingdom of God and his righteousness" (6:33). He asked them to "let your light shine before others, so that they may see your good works and give glory to your Father in heaven" (5:16). At the end Jesus told his followers, then and now, to "make disciples of all nations, baptizing them . . . and teaching them to obey everything that I have commanded you" (28:19-20). Perhaps this last directive of Jesus, usually called "the Great Commission," reminds us of the cultural mandate back in Genesis.[5] In short, Jesus invited all of his followers, including any of us today who believe in him, to participate in the kingdom as its agents, witnesses, and models. Perhaps "invited" is too mild a word. Jesus *elected* disciples to cure diseases, proclaim the good news of the kingdom, and bear "good fruit" (Luke 6:13; 9:1-2; John 15:16). In Scripture, people are elected not to feel good ("Look at me! I'm elected!") but to do good. Salvation is a gift of sheer grace, which God intends to flow through saved persons and out to others. "We are what he has made us, created in Christ Jesus for good works, which God prepared beforehand to be our way of life" (Eph. 2:10).

Given Jesus' summons, his followers have always understood that to be a "Christ person" is to be a "kingdom person." Working in the kingdom is our way of life. And many followers have concluded that we need powerful Christian education to learn how to serve the kingdom most intelligently.

---

5. I owe this point to Ronald J. Feenstra.

Vocation in the Kingdom of God

Let's call a person who accepts Jesus' commission a good citizen of the kingdom of God, and let's call a person who accepts this commission with enthusiasm a *prime* citizen of the kingdom. A good citizen likes the kingdom of God just fine, but a prime citizen passionately yearns for the kingdom. A prime citizen has been redeemed far down in her spirit, way downtown in her heart, so that she deeply loves God and the things of God. She relishes God's Word. She rejoices in God her Savior. She finds that the things of faith — repentance, forgiveness, hope in God — seem sweet to her. Her pulse quickens at the prospect of blessedness such as "no eye has seen, nor ear has heard, nor the human heart conceived" (1 Cor. 2:9). In her best moods she longs not just for happiness, but for joy; not just for joy, but for God; not just for God, but also for the kingdom of God. Because of her enthusiasm for the kingdom, she doesn't merely endorse justice in the world; she hungers and works for it. She doesn't merely reject cruelty; she hates and fights it. She wants God to make things right in the world, and she wants to enroll in God's project as if it were her own. She "strives first for the kingdom" in order to act on her passion.

In short, *she is a person with a calling.* She has been elected to be a follower of Jesus, which means she has been elected to serve the kingdom of God. A Christian's main vocation is to become a prime citizen of the kingdom of God — and this is true of every Christian, of artists and engineers as well as ministers and evangelists. All are called to mesh their kingdoms with those of other citizens in order to work together inside the kingdom of God.

How so? The first way is to belong to an active Christian church. In order to administer the kingdom, God has covenanted with particular people (the children of Israel, the New Testament church) to lead the way in saying and showing that God reigns. God uses the Christian church and her "means of grace" (preaching and sacraments, for instance) to spread the news about Jesus and the kingdom and to help people take the news to heart. Of all the ways that we can express

108

our citizenship in the kingdom of God, none is more obvious than becoming an active member of our local church.

Even if the Christian church is a primary instrument of the kingdom on earth, God also uses an array of other organizations to help the cause of the kingdom, each in its own sphere of influence. God uses national, intermediate, and local government to keep order and protect freedom — not an easy balance, as you can imagine, when some folks want peace and quiet in their neighborhood and other folks want lots of action there. Because government has enormous power to advance or retard human harmony and justice, Christians take a lively interest in it. John Calvin even regarded government as a sign of God's love for us, a means of grace, because it adjusts life in society toward civil righteousness and promotes "general peace and tranquility."[6] In an unguarded moment Calvin went so far as to declare that "civil authority is a calling, not only holy and lawful before God, but also the most sacred and by far the most honorable of all callings in the whole life of mortal men."[7] Though they might think Calvin got a little too breathless in his enthusiasm for civil authority, many Christians do think that a government job is an especially strategic post within the kingdom of God, and that cynicism or apathy about government therefore amounts to loss of faith in God's grace. Other Christians take a matter-of-fact view of civil authority (it's a necessary evil in a fallen world), and still others express real wariness about it, focusing on its power for evil. But most Christians believe that a citizen of the kingdom of God will take part in government — at minimum by voting intelligently, praying for leaders faithfully, and paying taxes willingly (I was going to write "cheerfully," but I knew you wouldn't buy that).

Besides government, God uses other institutions and groups to do some of the business of the kingdom, and Christians play their role in all of them. For instance, God uses industries to generate goods and services, hospitals to care for the hurt and sick, schools to

6. Calvin, *Institutes,* 2:1487 (4.20.2).
7. Calvin, *Institutes,* 2:1490 (4.20.4).

educate intellectual seekers, recreational clubs to remind us of the need for a Seventh Day to filter through all the rest of our days. God uses Habitat for Humanity to provide affordable housing for people who might otherwise never know what it's like to live in a castle. When we open our eyes, we'll find faithful Christians seeking to extend God's sovereignty in every country, in every precinct of life, including such tough precincts as advertising, journalism, university education, and the military.

Explicitly Christian groups and institutions will come right out and say that their goal is to serve the kingdom of God. In fact, the group will likely write this goal into their institutional literature, as in the case of Calvin College, whose mission statement says that the college "seeks to engage in vigorous liberal arts education that promotes lives of Christian service." This statement is not just wishful thinking or good public relations. It's a public witness and solemn vow. The generations of faithful men and women whose prayers, money, intelligence, and hope have combined in this college have wanted one

> *"The priest anoints you on the forehead and puts on you the sign [of the cross], in order that the enemy may turn away his eyes. . . . Henceforth from that day there is strife and counterstrife with him, and on this account the priest leads you into the spiritual arena as athletes of Christ by virtue of this anointing."*
>
> John Chrysostom[8]

8. St. John Chrysostom, *Baptismal Instructions*, trans. and ann. by Paul W. Harkins (Westminster, MD: The Newman Press, 1963), 52.

thing: they have wanted their college to "strive first for the kingdom of God" in the field of higher education.

But God needn't employ only Christian organizations to push forward the cause of his kingdom. God can use all kinds of groups and persons to further his purposes, including groups and persons that are uninterested in God or even opposed to God. This is striking. After all, as theologians from Augustine to Calvin to Kuyper have written, God is at war with what is anti-God. The kingdom of God and the kingdom of this world are sworn foes, one centering in the glory of God and the triumph of grace, and the other centering in the glory of the creature and the triumph of his autonomy. In this connection, Augustine referred to "two cities formed by two loves," and Kuyper to the "antithesis" between belief and unbelief. According to their thinking, ever since the fall, Jerusalem and Athens, Christ and Satan, the church and the world have been engaged in a lengthy and uneven clash whose outcome has already been determined by the death and resurrection of Christ. But the clash still shows up everywhere, and not the least in education, where opposing philosophies really do grapple with each other for the minds of students.

On the one hand, then, we have the clashing of the kingdoms. On the other hand, as we saw in Chapter 3, we have the surprising fact that, owing to the common grace of God, the world is often better than we expect. Thus, when it comes to caring for the earth, for example, non-Christians often lead the way, showing more enthusiasm for good earthkeeping than conservative Christians who claim that "the earth is the Lord's," but who don't act or vote that way.[9] It's true, of course, that some non-Christians want to care for the earth only because they tend toward materialist pantheism. Christians and Jews say, "the earth is the Lord's." Materialist pantheists say, "the earth is the Lord." But, ever the master of irony, God uses even the idolatrous philosophy of people who oppose him to get excellent earthkeeping out of them.

9. Scott Hoezee, *Remember Creation: God's World of Wonder and Delight* (Grand Rapids: Eerdmans, 1998), 91-94.

A prime citizen of the kingdom of God yearns for shalom, but non-Christians often yearn for at least a part of it too. Many non-Christians, even when they can't see Jesus Christ in their picture of "universal flourishing, wholeness, and delight" (the definition of shalom back in Chapter 1), still want freedom and justice. They still desire truth and beauty. Indeed, as I just suggested with respect to the environment, some non-Christians long so passionately for these realities, and work so tirelessly for them, that they put Christians to shame. A person does not have to believe in Christ in order, unconsciously, to do a part of Christ's work in the world. "All truth is God's truth," as the philosopher Arthur Holmes has said, following the teaching of Augustine, and the same may be said of justice and beauty. The same may be said of healthy hope and of common grace and of every other good thing. God is the *summum bonum,* not only because he is by nature incorruptibly good, but also because he is the overflowing *source* of good. As we noted earlier, even the opponents of God need the gifts of God. They need these gifts just to lead a tolerable life. In fact, they need the gifts of God — energy, intelligence, creativity — even to oppose God. The Holy Spirit of God blows where it

> I say móre: the just man justices;
> Keeps gráce: thát keeps all goings graces;
> Acts in God's eye what in God's eye he is —
> Christ — for Christ plays in ten thousand places,
> Lovely in limbs, and lovely in eyes not his . . .
>
> Gerard Manley Hopkins[10]

10. Gerard Manley Hopkins, "As Kingfishers Catch Fire," in *Poems and Prose of Gerard Manley Hopkins,* selected and with an intro. and notes by W. H. Gardner (New York: Penguin Books, 1953, reprint 1985).

wills among people and nations, and often the Spirit blows outside the congregations of the faithful.

Christians follow their main vocation by playing a lively part in institutions and endeavors that, consciously or not, seek the interests of the kingdom. Of these the church is first, but others — including governments, businesses, professions, and non-profit service organizations — are crucial as well. So are families. If they work right, families become a microcosm of the kingdom of God, incubating us in faith, hope, and love, schooling us in patience, supplying us with memories good enough to take out of storage on a lonely night. Families can give us our first lessons in meshing our kingdoms with others. They can fill us with delight, especially when they contain sunny, unspoiled toddlers.

> *"Still, when we ask ourselves which persons in our lives mean the most to us, we often find that it is those who, instead of giving much advice, solutions, or cures, have chosen rather to share our pain and touch our wounds with a gentle and tender hand. The friend who can be silent with us in a moment of despair or confusion, who can stay with us in an hour of grief and bereavement, who can tolerate not-knowing, not-curing, not-healing and face with us the reality of our powerlessness, that is the friend who cares."*
>
> Henri Nouwen[11]

11. Henri Nouwen, from *Out of Solitude: Three Meditations on the Christian Life* (Notre Dame, IN: Ave Maria, 1974), in *Seeds of Hope: A Henri Nouwen Reader,* ed. Robert Durback (New York: Bantam Books, 1989), 129.

To follow their main vocation of serving the kingdom of God, Christians pursue a wonderful array of sub-vocations. They sing, pray, and hand each other the body and blood of Christ. They rejoice with those who rejoice and weep with those who weep. They fight against evil, but also fly kites and bake bread. As part of their vocation they absorb good books and good music. They work, but also rest from work in order to make a space in which to long for God. Some of them join volunteer groups that turn rails to trails, or that assist flood victims, or that paint somebody's house. In an emergency, an adult Christian might spend herself for a friend who is dying — sitting with her, praying with her, encouraging her, seeing to some of her needs. This isn't a job that appears on any government list of occupations, but it is a calling of God, and it is surely a contribution to the kingdom of God.

Speaking of occupations, let's notice now that what we call "getting a job" or "going to work" is only one way of participating in the various interests of the kingdom. Volunteering to teach Sunday school is another. So is stepping into a voting booth and making conscientious choices there. So is deciding whether to marry or to remain single, and, if married, whether to conceive or adopt children, or do both. These are all *vocational* decisions for a citizen of the kingdom, and some of them are large. But a Christian looks at even the smaller decisions (who deserves my support for the office of county drain commissioner?) with faith and good humor, aware that in the plan of God, the mustard seed of one of our decisions may combine with the mustard seeds of others' decisions to bring good growth for the kingdom.

Here we must avoid a common temptation to think of our vocation as no more than our job or career and to think of college as mere job training. It's easy to think that college is preparatory school for becoming, say, a dentist, or a city planner, or an elementary school teacher. According to this way of thinking, professors, college staff members, and parents or others who help with tuition — all these people are there mainly to help us get a good job.

Not so. Of course, professors and others will be pleased if you get a good job. Good work is worth doing, and the world needs plenty of people who do it well. Moreover, a superb education at your Christian college or university will indeed make you employable in respectable places. But thinking of college as no more than job training is a narrow-minded impoverishment of the kingdom of God. That's like thinking that a flight attendant needs to be an alert person mainly to remember people's drink orders. Of course, alertness does come in handy when it comes time to take and fill an order. But that's not the only, and not even the central, reason why a flight attendant ought to be alert.

So let's think again about your college education. Your degree will certainly make you more employable, but, so far as the kingdom is concerned, that's only one dimension of the value of your education. The full value of your education is that it will help you find and prepare for your vocation — which, as we've just seen, is much bigger than any particular occupation. In fact, you might retire from a very different occupation than the one in which you started, and you might have tried several others in the interim. (As one of my colleagues likes to say, "God's other name is 'Surprise.'") In any event, your college education is meant to prepare you for prime citizenship in the kingdom of God. For four years or so, such preparation is itself a big part of your vocation. Your calling is to prepare for further calling, and to do so in a Christian college community that cares as much about the kind of person you are becoming as what kind of job you will eventually get, and as much about *how* you will do your job as about *which* job you do.

Still, career choices do matter, and college is a natural place to think about them. God does endow us with particular gifts and interests that better equip us for kingdom service in some fields than in others. Not all of us have what it takes to be ballet dancers, for example. We're not tough enough.

Most North American college students consider various career paths while they are still in school, and many invest a good deal of energy in finding a path that seems right for them. A Christian does too. But a Christian may approach such a decision in faith and without

115

> "The place God calls you to is the place where your deep gladness and the world's deep hunger meet."
>
> Frederick Buechner[12]

the panicky feeling that "I've *got* to get this degree to be competitive." A Christian has more poise. Like everybody else, she'll assess her gifts and interests. She'll think of what kind of work she could do naturally, in sync with her temperament and approaches to life. She'll study the job market. Like others, she will probably notice how lucrative and prestigious her potential career might be, especially if she thinks of entering a demanding profession. But if she's "striving first for the kingdom" she will deliberately bracket considerations of big money and prestige in favor of more important issues.

To "strive first for the kingdom" in choosing a career, a Christian will ask himself particular questions. Where in the kingdom does God want me to work? Where are the needs great? Where are the workers few? Where are the temptations manageable? With whom would I work? How honest is

> "When Christ calls a man, he bids him come and die."
>
> Dietrich Bonhoeffer[13]

the work I'm thinking of doing? How necessary and how healthy are the goods or services I would help provide? How smoothly could I combine my proposed career with being a spouse, if that's also my calling, or a parent, or a faithful child of aging parents? How close would I be to a church in which I could give and take nourishment? Is my proposed career inside a system so corrupt that, even with the best intentions, I would end up absorbing a lot more evil than I conquer?

12. Frederick Buechner, *Wishful Thinking: A Seeker's ABC,* rev. and expanded (San Francisco: HarperSanFrancisco, 1993), 119.
13. Dietrich Bonhoeffer, *The Cost of Discipleship* (New York: Simon & Schuster, 1995), 89. I owe the juxtaposition of the Buechner and Bonhoeffer quotes to L. Gregory Jones.

Placing emphasis where Jesus placed it, a prime citizen will add another question: What would my career do for "the least of these"?

What all of these questions express is an interest in serving the common good. God has ordered human society in such a way that we all depend on each other. Before we give thanks for our daily bread, somebody has to have baked it. In fact, before a slice of honey oatmeal appears on our plate, a number of farmers, millers, bakers, distributors, drivers, grocers, and others have had to work together in order to supply our need. This is a commercial arrangement, but not *only* a commercial arrangement. As Lee Hardy has written, it's also a social arrangement that expresses and reinforces our dependence on each other. God *intends* "that human beings should live in a society bound together by common needs and mutual service."[14] In fact, our dependence on each other is so profound, and so much a part of the meshing of our kingdoms inside God's kingdom, that when Jesus wanted to illustrate how to receive the kingdom of God he pointed to a baby. "Whoever does not receive the kingdom of God as a little child will never enter it," he said (Luke 18:17). Jesus almost surely meant that before we ever have anything to give, before we're ever ready to build a barn or dig a well, we have to learn how to become good *receivers*. Infants don't do much. They just lie around all day. But they are perfectly wonderful receivers, and therefore they are our teachers when it comes to one of the relationships — dependence — that ties us to each other and to God.

God Loveth Adverbs

At the end of the last chapter we saw that God's program of redemption is all-encompassing. Wherever life has been corrupted, it needs to be reformed. Accordingly, a prime citizen of the kingdom will typically be a reform-minded citizen, looking for ways to address some of the deformities in human life and culture. As you know, reform hap-

---

14. Lee Hardy, *The Fabric of This World: Inquiries into Calling, Career Choice, and the Human Design of Work* (Grand Rapids: Eerdmans, 1990), 60.

pens in many ways. It may occur when a nation gets shamed into seeing its injustice (think of civil rights legislation) or its carelessness (think of new building codes that require wheelchair accessibility). It may occur when the conscientious efforts of good people in business, medicine, law, labor, education, and elsewhere gain sufficient momentum so as to make a positive difference in those fields.

Some of these reforms are led by Christian people who genuinely hope for the kingdom of God. Some are led by non-Christian people moved by a simple desire for truth or justice. Many are led by people with mixed motives. But every genuine advance toward shalom is led by the Holy Spirit, who promiscuously chooses instruments of God's peace. In any case, Christian people seek the gift of discernment to know when and how to join existing movements toward shalom and when and how to start new ones.

But here a word of caution is in order. It's one thing to talk about reform, and another to do it. Christians have been good at talking, and writing, and talking some more. And some have been pretty good at doing, too. But it's possible for reform-minded people to overestimate their rhetoric and underestimate the job. Some social realities are extremely resistant to reform. Great money, power, or pleasure supports them. Great acceptance surrounds them. Long traditions sustain them. Some of these realities therefore seem irredeemable, or nearly so. Racism, for example, is an evil of great staying power. People may reform their speech and practice where racial relations are concerned, but the reforms don't always stick, and sometimes they don't make it all the way through to people's hearts. Or people reform for a while and then backslide. Moreover, racism can work its way from people's hearts into the structure of institutions, where it is sometimes hard to get at. Or, besides racism, take an old problem of which you may have recent memories: What would have to happen for high school students to quit forming into cliques that marginalize or even terrorize their weak or unpopular classmates?

John Calvin believed that an unredeemed life keeps oscillating back and forth between pride ("I've made it!") and despair ("I'll never

> *"One of the most blasphemous consequences of injustice, especially racist injustice, is that it can make a child of God doubt that he or she is a child of God."*
>
> Desmond Mpilo Tutu[15]

make it"). In his view, redemption gives people security, or (one of Calvin's favorite words) *repose*. His idea was that those who lean into God's grace and let it hold them up can then drop some of their performance anxiety.

Perhaps the same pattern holds for Christians' approach to reforming culture. On the one hand, we need to avoid triumphalism, the prideful view that we Christians will fully succeed in transforming all or much of culture. No doubt triumphalists underestimate some of the difficulties. They may underestimate cultural ironies too. After all, the history of the world is full of revolutions that Christians hailed as part of the coming of God's kingdom, only to discover that the revolutions ended up generating as much tyranny as they displaced.

On the other hand, we also need to avoid the despairing tendency to write the world off, to abandon it as a lost cause, and to remove ourselves to an island of like-minded Christians. The world, after all, belongs to God and is in the process of being redeemed by God. "God so loved the world that he gave his only Son . . . in order that the world might be saved through him" (John 3:16-17). Indeed, God's plan is to gather up *all things* in Christ. How bizarre it would be for Christians to turn their backs on this plan. How ungrateful it would be to receive the bread of life and then refuse to share it with others.

As a matter of fact, Christians have been put in a solid position

15. Desmond Mpilo Tutu, *No Future without Forgiveness* (New York: Doubleday, 1999), 197.

where the reform of culture is concerned: we have been invited to live beyond triumphalism and despair, spending ourselves for a cause that we firmly believe will win in the end. So, on the one hand, we don't need to take responsibility for trying to fix everything. The earth is the Lord's, and he will save it. On the other hand, we may take responsibility for contributing what we uniquely *have* to contribute to the kingdom, joining with many others from across the world who are striving to be faithful, to add the work of their hands and minds to the eventual triumph of God.

Meanwhile, none of us is stuck with trying to promote the kingdom of God with an occupation we can't stand. At one time people were born into their occupations, so that the son of a farmer, for example, was simply expected to take over the family farm. If he wanted to do something else with his life he was thought to be peculiar or, worse, traitorous. But, as Nicholas Wolterstorff has written, Reformed Christians of the sixteenth and seventeenth centuries rejected the old idea that each of us is born to be just one thing — a butcher, a baker, a candlestick maker. Instead, each of us must find an occupation so intrinsically valuable and so naturally suited to us that, through it, we may add to the treasure of the kingdom. In fact, adds Wolterstorff, we must not only find an occupation to bring to the kingdom; we must *shape* it to suit this purpose.[16] The point is that occupations are often valuable to the kingdom, but only if we reform them. So in today's world, perhaps a Christian would shape the occupation of quality-control supervisor by encouraging whistle-blowers instead of retaliating against them. Perhaps a Christian would shape the occupation of computer repair technician by doing top-notch diagnoses in order to save customers the expense of unnecessary repairs. Perhaps a Christian would shape the occupation of CEO of a major airline by telling its customers the truth about flight cancellations and delays. In any case, occupational reforms serve the kingdom of God as surely as a Billy Graham Crusade does.

Only a few of us will launch great reform movements, and even

16. Wolterstorff, *Justice and Peace*, 17.

fewer of us will do it deliberately. But all of us may offer our gifts and energies to the cause of God's program in the world. When we make this offering by means of an ordinary occupation, we will sometimes feel as if our *lives* are very ordinary. No matter. An ordinary occupation done conscientiously builds the kingdom of God. Jesus built the kingdom as a carpenter before he built it as a rabbi. And he taught us in the parable of the talents that the question for disciples is not *which* callings they have but how faithfully they pursue them. In remarking on this theme, the Puritan Joseph Hall wrote:

> The homeliest service that we doe in an honest calling, though it be but to plow, or digge, if done in obedience, and conscience of God's Commandement, is crowned with an ample reward; whereas the best workes for their kinde (preaching, praying, offering Evangelicall sacrifices) if without respect of God's injunction and glory, are loaded with curses. God loveth adverbs; and cares not how good, but how well.[17]

Vocation and Education

A college education can help a Christian follow his vocation, including its occupational component. Secular higher education is also one of the tools God can use for this purpose, but it's often a blunt one. Mainstream education isn't set up to help students form a Christian philosophy of life and vocation, including a philosophy of good and evil derived from sustained reflection on the drama of creation, fall, and redemption. In fact, it's common in postmodern secular education to reject all "meta-narratives" of the kind that the biblical story represents — that is, stories that transcend their own cultural setting and purport to be universally true. (What could be more presumptuous, postmodernists think, than to suppose that the biblical account

17. Quoted in Charles H. George and Katherine George, *The Protestant Mind of the English Reformation* (Princeton: Princeton University, 1961), 139n.

of creation, fall, and redemption explains *human* life, and not just the lives of Bible believers!) In secular academia, religious approaches to learning are generally unwelcome — sometimes dismissed, but more often simply ignored. Thus it would be unusual in an Ivy League classroom to find a discussion of spiral and elliptical galaxies that referred not only to their beauty and immensity but also to the even greater beauty and immensity of their Creator. It would be rare to find a discussion of economic relations that focused on the spiritual significance of poverty or of consumerism.[18] It would be uncommon in a discussion of racism to find it rejected because it fails to honor the image of God in other human beings. The biblical account of God's creation of all human beings in his image is, after all, another of those forbidden meta-narratives.

Predictably enough, secular education tends to promote a secular view of the world and of human life, routinely giving students the impression that theistic accounts of reality have become passé, that they aren't important enough to be considered, that educated people don't think about them much. Moreover, secular education is plagued by various falsehoods and confusions that have become fashionable in postmodernity — that God is dead, or, alternatively, that God interferes with human autonomy and ought to stop; that there isn't any such thing as truth; that it is wicked to make moral judgments (think that one over); that our main aim as human beings is self-expression or even self-deification; that right and wrong are whatever anybody thinks they are; that power trumps all else; and so on.[19]

Christian students on secular campuses may expect to stand against these ideas without caving in to them and without hardening into pious anti-intellectuals. If so, they expect a lot. And if they expect to develop a mature Christian philosophy of life without the help of

18. In "Religion-free Texts: Getting an Illiberal Education," *Christian Century*, July 14-21, 1999, 711-15, Warren A. Nord demonstrates that public high school textbooks "systematically exclude religious voices." Many of his observations apply to secular education more generally, including secular higher education.

19. Alvin Plantinga, *Warranted Christian Belief* (New York: Oxford University, 2000), 423.

their professors — in fact, with the *hindrance* of some of their professors — they expect even more. I acknowledge that an unusual Christian student might rise to the challenge. He might telephone people for help, read books outside of class, join InterVarsity Christian Fellowship, consult with the campus chaplain in the hope that she could offer him a small co-curriculum of Christian Perspectives on Learning. He might join an organization specifically designed to think Christianly about major campus topics, such as the superb Veritas Forum at Harvard University, which helps Christian students "lay Christ in the bottome." He might even have the courage to try out his faith in class. His idea would be that you can dare to be a Daniel only if you spend time in the lions' den, and his idea is definitely worth considering. In fact, every Christian community includes some Daniels who made it through the academic dens of confusion and conformity with their kingdom vocation intact and sometimes even purified by the fires of adversity.

But I fear that for most Christian students mainstream higher education simply won't be adequate to help them understand the kingdom of God and their own vocation within it. Such students will be busy with a hundred other things and won't take the time or spend the effort to sort out the good and evil in what they encounter on campus and to construct a thoughtful Christian philosophy of life on their own. They will find it easier to go with the flow, sometimes aware of dissonances between their faith and their learning and between their faith and their campus life, sometimes unaware that they are absorbing views of the world and of life that flatly contradict the gospel. Content with personal prayer, personal witnessing, and small-group Bible study as ways of being Christian on campus, a number of these students will live with a wall between their sacred faith and their secular learning.

The sponsors of strongly Christian colleges and universities have tried to imagine "a more excellent way." They have designed a program of higher education that refuses to separate the sacred from the secular, believing that the Christian faith must be woven through the life of learning so that there, as everywhere else, Jesus Christ is Lord.

My own college said as much in 1997 when it adopted a Statement of Purpose for its new core curriculum:

> Christians seek to live their whole lives in continuity with Christ, taking on his mind and affections, acting as his body in the world, sharing his sufferings and his victories in the project of overcoming misery and rebuilding God's good creation. Christians gladly join this project out of gratitude to Christ, out of obedience to Christ, and out of an enkindled desire to work within the Kingdom of Christ. As faithful workers within this Kingdom, Christians struggle to align themselves with the redemptive purposes of God in this world.[20]

Education at a Christian college is meant to demonstrate this "continuity with Christ" and therefore to line up "with the redemptive purposes of God in the world." Or put it like this: your Christian college education is designed to help you love the Lord our God with all your *mind,* and then to love your neighbor as yourself with a life of educated service. In this way, your Christian higher education may serve both as your present vocation and as your preparation for a life-long vocation as a prime citizen of the kingdom.

How so? How does Christian higher education work? What's the process?

Day to day, the process is one of gaining the knowledge, skills, and virtues you will need to make your contribution to the kingdom of God. Faculty, staff, and other students will help you acquire these things.

But a word of caution: just as it would be a huge mistake simply to go with the flow on a secular campus, so it's a huge mistake to suppose you can get truly educated by floating downstream in a Christian college. An education is something you have to achieve; it's almost something you have to win. I mean that a seasoned Christian

20. Preface to "An Engagement with God's World: A Statement of Purpose for the Core Curriculum of Calvin College."

approach to the world and human life requires a real struggle with alternative approaches. A maturing Christian has to think about them, wonder about them, try to see what's attractive and partly true in them. If you have chosen a Christian college so you won't have to wrestle with Nietzsche or worry about evolution, you've come to the wrong school. You can't "rise with Christ" unless you've died with him first, and that means enduring some dark nights of the soul.

The disciples could not "watch with me even one hour," as Jesus lamented, and it has always been a temptation for Christian students (and their parents) to want a safe college where there are no intellectual or existential Gethsemanes. But this is an illusion. It may even be a kind of cowardice. The truth is that a student who is trying — under sure-handed supervision — to learn a mature Christian approach to the world will have to take some pain, including the pain of doubt or of indecision. In fact, if you are a doubter, the Bible is your book. It's full of the doubts and laments of believers whose faith emerges only from a crucible of some kind. Jesus' own lament from the cross, "My God, my God, why have you forsaken me?" (Mark 15:34) has become one of the most famous things he said, a small death during his big death.

Followers of Jesus struggle not only with their work but also with their prayers, with their meditations, with attempting to open spaces at the depths where the Spirit of God may descend and dwell. The

> *"And the thought came to me, sudden and shocking, that the broken and contrite heart is something far more terrible than penitence."*
>
> Alan Paton[21]

21. Alan Paton, *Too Late the Phalarope* (New York: Simon & Schuster, 1995), 275.

spiritual disciplines (prayer, study, meditation, confession) look as if they would be a pain; and they are. But they are also a joy. They look as if they would bind us. They do, but they bind our own internal constraints — the desires that lead us around if we do not bind them. So the disciplines actually open a door to freedom. The discipline of study can feel like a burden. It is a burden, but the Christian person yokes up with Jesus Christ to haul the burden, and the joy and freedom of fellowship with Christ make the burden light. In short, the disciplines help make us prime citizens of the kingdom because they help to make us strong and deep.

As a person with responsible dominion in the world, you will need to take responsibility for your own education, *seeing to it* that you gain the knowledge, hone the skills, and develop the virtues you'll need now and later in order to play your role in the drama of the kingdom. At my own college (sorry to refer to it again, but it's the one I know best) our Statement of Purpose for the Core Curriculum includes a full treatment of these components. Here's a sampling, largely from that document, of the knowledge, skills, and virtues you'll need in some combination in order to find and follow your vocation.

> "Superficiality is the curse of our age. The doctrine of instant satisfaction is a primary spiritual problem. The desperate need today is not for a greater number of intelligent people, or gifted people, but for deep people."
>
> Richard J. Foster[22]

22. Richard J. Foster, *Celebration of Discipline: The Path to Spiritual Growth* (San Francisco: Harper & Row, 1978), 1.

Knowledge

We want a body of knowledge in order to love God intellectually, as well as every other way, and also in order to identify and address human needs, including our own. For these purposes we need knowledge of the triune God; of creation, fall, and redemption; of the tenets and practices of the Christian religion — all of this knowledge leading naturally to the development of a "Christian world-and-life view." (Thus the need for books of the kind you're reading.) With such a view, and with increasing knowledge of the natural world, human society, history, the arts, and our own identities and callings, a Christian student will be able at some point to take an educated position on such issues and questions as these:

- how the world's other major religions might simultaneously express serious confusions and also the *sensus divinitatis* with which God has endowed the whole human race;
- whether history is the sad tale of decline from an old golden age, or the heartening story of progress toward a new one, or (depending on how these ages are understood) both, or neither;
- how quantitative structures represent not only "the alphabet in which God wrote the universe" but also a primary alphabet of social research methods and of public policy;
- why land (sandy seashores, let's say) shapes human culture, and why human culture shapes land, and what these shapings might have to do with responsible dominion;
- Whether economic growth in the capitalist economy of a developing nation is likely to be cruel or kind or both;
- what it means to belong to a community in covenant with God;
- why a work of art might ennoble life in one way and degrade it in another;
- how to explain the rise of mall-speak among North American middle school students ("He goes '*Yes!*' and I'm, like, 'Whoa!'") and how to assess its significance.

Skills

Beyond a body of knowledge, a student also needs to acquire, or sharpen, an array of skills. These enable a student to prevail not only in class and on campus but also in a host of vocational settings throughout life. Skills are "how to" disciplines that, like all disciplines, require a certain amount of sweat and repetition, and then yield some wonderful freedoms. (Think, for example, of a jazz musician improvising on a rhythmic or melodic theme and of the combination of discipline and freedom that's displayed in the improvisation.)

An educated Christian student will possess some combination of such skills as these. She'll know how to:

- construct and test an argument for a thesis;
- argue without quarreling;
- read and correlate tables of statistics and judge their relevance to a proposed business plan;
- use a Versaport Slider;
- spot an idol;

> "My brother, Cecil Edward Chesterton, was born when I was about five years old; and, after a brief pause, began to argue. He continued to argue to the end. . . . I am glad to think that through all those years we never stopped arguing; and we never once quarrelled. Perhaps the principal objection to a quarrel is that it interrupts an argument."
>
> G. K. Chesterton[23]

23. G. K. Chesterton, *Autobiography* (London: Hutchinson, 1937), 196.

> *"The approach to style is by way of plainness, simplicity, orderliness, sincerity. . . . Muddiness is not merely a disturber of prose, it is also a destroyer of life, of hope."*
>
> E. B. White[24]

- read Scripture passages in context;
- write a clear sentence and sometimes a lively one;
- identify and interpret tropes;
- understand and speak a second language;
- form and follow a sound research plan;
- square up for a shot;
- play an arpeggio in tune;
- speak a strengthening word to a discouraged prof without angling for a better grade.

A little reflection tells us that Christians want such skills not to impress the less skillful and not simply to become more employable. Christians hope to increase the net amount of shalom in the world. Thus, a clearly written sentence not only conveys a thought or raises a question; it also saves readers from unnecessary confusion. A well-executed piece of team defense not only leads toward victory; it also delights viewers who understand its intelligence. Learning a second language not only equips a person to pursue business or art in new venues; it also respects strangers and opens the way for hospitality to them.[25] Along these lines, knowledge and skills often enable a person

24. E. B. White, "An Approach to Style," in William Strunk and E. B. White, *The Elements of Style* (New York: Macmillan, 1959), 57 and 65 respectively.

25. For this last possibility see Barbara M. Carvill and David I. Smith, *The Gift of the Stranger: Faith, Hospitality, and Foreign Language Learning* (Grand Rapids: Eerdmans, 2000).

to express not only the critical discernment of a prophet but also the committed heart of a servant.

Virtues

Classical education has always encouraged students to acquire more than knowledge and skills; it has also encouraged them to develop the virtues that will incline them to use these things for the benefit of others. Christians believe that such virtues derive from the Holy Spirit and that this is so no matter who has them. But, as we saw in Chapter 4, Christians have special reason for cultivating honesty, compassion, and other good traits. These virtues suit Christians. They're part of dying and rising with Christ and therefore part of the family uniform for the people of God. It's extremely *fitting* for those who have received grace at so great a cost to offer it to others, and by doing so to build up not only the church, but also the kingdom of God.

Once more, consider these words from Calvin College's Statement of Purpose for the Core Curriculum:

> Virtues are settled dispositions to feel and act in certain ways. A compassionate person is inclined, as if by nature, to be moved by human suffering. A person in possession of the virtue of honesty has the disposition to tell the truth. Vices are also dispositions. A callous person, bearing within the breast a heart of stone, disregards the needs of others as a matter of habit. A person saddled with the vice of deceitfulness has the disposition to lie whenever lying seems convenient. A particular array of virtues and vices, taken together, makes up a person's character.[26]

Let's be clear about the nature of dispositions. A compassionate person is one who not only *doesn't* close his heart to human suffering;

26. "An Engagement with God's World."

130

he *wouldn't* do so. An honest person not only *doesn't* lie or steal; she *wouldn't* do these things. If she ever did, she would feel out of sync, out of step with herself. A virtuous person needs rules the way a golfer needs "checkpoints" in squaring himself up for a good tee shot. He needs the checkpoints to learn a solid setup for a shot, but after many repetitions a person makes a practice of feeling and doing what's right. He "has a habit" where virtue is concerned, and so he naturally does what's right.

In a Christian college we learn and practice virtues in ways that fit into the dynamic process of teaching and learning, the process of preparation for the several dimensions of a life's calling. We learn such virtues as

- diligence, the inclination to dig in for the long haul, to "keep on keeping on" in the face of intellectual obstacles or other difficulties;
- patience, the readiness to absorb irritants without letting them paralyze us;

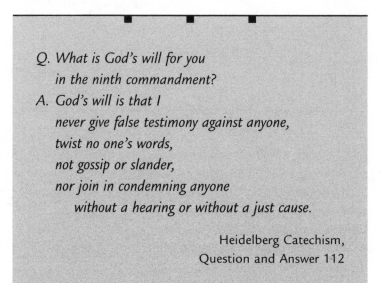

Q. What is God's will for you
   in the ninth commandment?
A. God's will is that I
   never give false testimony against anyone,
   twist no one's words,
   not gossip or slander,
   nor join in condemning anyone
      without a hearing or without a just cause.

Heidelberg Catechism,
Question and Answer 112

131

- charity, the inclination to give others — including authors we dislike — the benefit of the doubt, putting the best face on their words and motives;
- stewardship, the disposition to take good care not only of the world's resources but also of our own, so that we students, faculty, and staff spend time, money, energy, and intelligence on pursuits that really do answer God's calling, and not just our own whims.

"Character is destiny," said the ancient Greek thinker Heraclitus. How we feel and act in classrooms and labs, on stages and playing fields, with friends and strangers will lead us toward one future rather than another. The charitable person, for example, will discover friends among those that the uncharitable person simply dismisses. The truth-telling person will move good projects forward because she has traction on reality. The patient person will always be hard to defeat and will therefore often win through to first-class achievements.

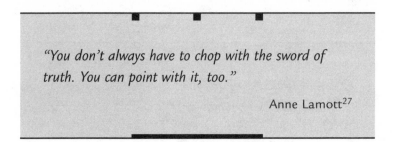

"You don't always have to chop with the sword of truth. You can point with it, too."

Anne Lamott[27]

In fact, when a well-educated person combines knowledge, skills, and virtues to pursue God's calling — whether or not he is conscious of it — the result may be remarkable. I could cite a number of examples, but consider just one that has to do with your vision.

Given the number of maladies that can afflict it — whether because of a retinal defect or because of the brain's misapprehending

---

27. Anne Lamott, *Bird by Bird* (New York: Doubleday, 1995), 156.

what the eye is perceiving — it's amazing that any one of us should have 20/20, Kodak-color vision without corrective lenses.

In the early 1980s, Dr. Helen Irlen was conducting research on adults who'd been diagnosed with dyslexia. The results of her research soon presented a pattern among some: those who preferred to read in dim light also said they preferred not to read black print on white paper. Instead they favored, say, black words on red paper or purple paper — some color that was less of a contrast to the black. When the contrast was great, they said, words on a page faded in or out, or leaped around, or became like islands in a delta with little white rivers flowing between them.[28]

While most of the people in her study said that they experienced this phenomenon only while they were reading, a few noted that they endured bizarre visual distortions all the time. They felt as if they lived in an animated "house of mirrors" where sidewalks buckled, buildings folded, and fire hydrants needed a leash. Using computer imaging, one young woman, Alex, was able to re-create her symptoms of "scotopic sensitivity" so that Dr. Irlen could better understand it. Eventually Dr. Irlen discovered that if Alex wore glasses tinted just the right shade of blue, Alex's animated world ceased its assault.

Today tinted lenses are used to correct the vision of thousands who suffer from dyslexia, scotopic sensitivity, or color blindness. In each case, a simple tinted lens "tricks" the brain into reinterpreting what the eye says it sees. By combining knowledge, skill, and virtue, Dr. Irlen developed an imaginative address to three maladies, and thereby served the kingdom of God.

How good it is when human beings serve in such ways. How wonderful it is when they do it in conscious acknowledgment of the calling of God and in faith that, between this life and the next, between the partial coming of the kingdom and the full coming of the kingdom, nothing good will ever be lost.

28. Paul R. Whiting, "How Difficult Can Reading Be?" *Parent & Citizen* 44, no. 4 (1993): 12-18.

Epilogue

■ ■ ■ ■ ■

The earth is the LORD*'s and all that is in it,*
the world, and those who live in it.

Psalm 24:1

God blessed Noah and his sons, and said to them, "Be fruit-
ful, and multiply, and fill the earth. . . . I establish my cove-
nant with you, that . . . never again shall there be a flood to
destroy the earth."

Genesis 9:1, 11

"Then they will see 'the Son of Man coming in a cloud' with
power and great glory."

Luke 21:27-28

Then I saw a new heaven and a new earth . . . and I saw the
holy city, the new Jerusalem, coming down out of heaven
from God. . . . And I heard a loud voice from the throne say-
ing, "See, the home of God is among mortals."

Revelation 21:1-3a

I've been writing all along that education is for service in the kingdom of God — or for shalom in God's kingdom. Our education matters, and I now want to add that it matters not only for this world but also for the world to come. My reason for thinking so is that Scripture appears to teach not only that there shall be a new heaven and earth, but also that it shall be *this* earth, renewed. In Revelation 21 the city of God descends to us. We do not go to heaven; heaven comes to us. In a vision lovely enough to break a person's heart, John shows us what God showed him, that up ahead of us, after centuries of tribal feuds and racial arrogance, after centuries of xenophobic snapping at each other, after we human beings have silted history full with the debris of all our antagonisms — after all that, the city of God will descend to us, and God will dwell with us, and, once more, God will make all things new.

The Old Testament prophecies of shalom — of perfect justice, harmony, and delight among God, human beings, and all creation — are interpreted in various ways by various Christians. My own view is that they apply neither to the present church (of which in any case they are not true) nor to a future existence in a distant, airy heaven. These prophecies apply to the future of a very solid, tangible, visible earth.[1] Or to the earth and a number of other planets. On this view, Fripp Island, S.C., will be a part of heaven. So will the Lake District in England, the Schwarzwald of southwest Germany, and the Great Barrier Reef off the eastern coast of Australia. Banff will be included, and the islands of Indonesia. Kenya's game preserves will still draw visitors, and so will the mountains of northeast Korea.

In this vision, one can spot lines of continuity between the work of Christ in the present and in the future, between the small whispers and hints now and the final cosmic renewal and triumph of the Lamb. What we do now in the name of Christ — striving for healing, for justice, for intellectual light in darkness, striving simply to produce something helpful for sustaining the lives of other human be-

1. Anthony A. Hoekema, *The Bible and the Future* (Grand Rapids: Eerdmans, 1979), 281-87.

ings — shall be preserved across into the next life. All of it counts, all of it lasts, none of it is wasted or lost. All of it acts like salt that eventually seasons a whole slab of meat, or a seed that grows one day into a tree that looks nothing like the seed at all.

For there is both cultural continuity and transformation in the link between this world and the next. As we know, twisted culture now fills the earth. God's mandate to "multiply and fill the earth" has been answered too often by strip mines, oil slicks, and denuded rain forests; too often by dictatorships and ethnic cleansing; too often by computerized dope distribution schemes. Great scientists use their excellent minds to dream up weapons that find their way into the hands of terrorists. Television writers put a good face on godlessness. Ministers use their seminary training to preach gospels in which all the difficult bits about sin and grace have been purposely razored away. "Multiply and fill the earth," said God after the flood. And the earth is now full. The trouble is that it's full of our trash as well as God's treasure.

Remarkably, God wants the earth anyhow. God wants it back. Why? What's the point? The earth's trash is, after all, the product of our fallenness, of our disobedience. It's the product and encouragement of human arrogance. Why doesn't God flush it all away with another deluge?

Because God has promised to preserve the earth. As you recall, Genesis 9 records God's promise never again to destroy the earth with a flood. The point is that the earth is the Lord's. The point is that the earth *in all its fullness* is the Lord's. God means to reclaim the fullness that is his. But just as you and I have to be converted, so does all of culture. Swords will have to be turned back into pruning shears, switchblades into paring knives, and spears into garden hoes. High-powered dope-running speedboats — cigarette boats — will have to be reclaimed for teaching poor children to water-ski. In the new heaven and earth, intercontinental ballistic missile silos will be transformed into training tanks for scuba divers.[2]

2. Richard J. Mouw, *When the Kings Come Marching In: Isaiah and the New Jerusalem* (Grand Rapids: Eerdmans, 1983), 16-20.

In a thousand ways, God will gather what's scattered, rebuild what's broken, restore what has been emptied out by centuries of waste and fraud. In a thousand ways, God will put right what's wrong with his glorious creation. In fact, the Bible hints that the new heaven and earth may *surpass* the original creation: marriage, for instance, will no longer be necessary for human fellowship at its deepest level (Mark 12:25).

The earth is the Lord's, in all its fullness. We have corrupted the earth through folly and sin, but God means to restore all things in the harmony, justice, and delight of shalom. This is a sign to us: On the third day Jesus Christ rose again from the dead, the pledge that one day all things shall be renewed. And God has called people like us to become agents for the restoration project that is already in process. These agents need to be educated. More than we could ever think or say, Christian education is for this project. Christian education is the training of special agents of the kingdom of God and the consummation of creation. That's why you are at your Christian college or university. That's why all of us — students, faculty, staff, administrators — spend our time, spend our money, spend ourselves in Christian higher education.

Meanwhile, don't imagine that while you're in college you're in some kind of holding tank awaiting the great day when you'll emerge into the "real world." People will speak of college life to you in this way, saying things like, "Just wait till you get to the *real* world." Often what they mean is "just wait till you get out here where balancing work and leisure is nearly impossible and keeping up with debts is a real headache." If that's the "real world," then you're already in it.

But jobs, bills, and stress aren't necessarily the "real world" either, or at least not anything like the whole of it. To think in that way is to think small. No matter what our primary occupation, we can't let it become a preoccupation. Even now, when we get really focused on cramming for tests and cranking out papers, it's easy to let the rest of reality fade into the background. Soon the world is no bigger than our dorm room, a classroom, and the sidewalks in between. And that's not the real world at all.

Someone who lives in the "real world" lives with an awareness of the *whole* world, because the *whole* world is part of the kingdom of God. On any given day he may walk no more than a mile, but his imagination will trot the globe.

While you're at college, I hope you'll find it perfectly natural to let your mind purposely wander in this way, wondering about life abroad, perhaps keeping a globe or an atlas handy. One obvious way to become directly acquainted with the world is to immerse yourself in another culture for a time. Many Christian colleges provide opportunities to study abroad. Try to take advantage of one of them. Maybe you'll travel to the Galapagos Islands to study tropical flora and fauna and to see how conservationists are preserving the delicate ecosystem there. Or maybe one fall you'll spend a semester in Hungary, exploring the history, culture, and politics of a Central European nation that's struggling for identity in the post–Cold War era. Or maybe you'll live in Honduras for a semester, gaining firsthand experience of third-world poverty and of development efforts designed to relieve it. Having studied abroad, students often report that their experience has expanded and complicated their understanding of the kingdom of God in ways they could never have guessed. Often they report that their hope for the new heaven and earth has picked up speed. Some students find that studying abroad forever changes their lives.

Then again, maybe you're already immersing yourself in another culture simply by coming to college. Maybe you've flown through the airspace of fifteen different countries on three different continents and had your passport checked a half-dozen times before you even arrived in the United States. If you are an international student, you bring the world to us North Americans in a way that the news and *National Geographic* never could. Sometimes we'll be shy about asking you questions, afraid of exposing our ignorance. Still, while you're exploring North American culture, we hope you'll give us more than a glimpse of your own country's culture, broadening our horizons even as you broaden your own.

International travel is wonderful, but it's not the only — nor the most expedient — way to stir our imaginations and increase our knowledge of the world. That's why many educated people pick up a credible newspaper every day, either on-line or off the stand. Maybe the best we can do in a busy week is scan the headlines. Even so, we'll spot some part of the drama of the kingdom that is destined to come one day in all its fullness.

The same opportunities present themselves in much of the curriculum and co-curriculum at Christian colleges and universities. The same is true of student organizations, whether they grapple with contemporary issues, produce entertainment, or explore a profession. Campus worship expresses the drama of the kingdom every day, as we join the voices of Christians from around the world and throughout all of history to extol our Creator, to intercede for his people, and to anticipate future glory. Campus publications, concerts, plays, lectures, and art gallery exhibits all help to expand and enrich our engagement with God's world.

In each of these places and events, something of creation, fall, and redemption comes to us. In each of these venues we encounter the real world through some medium. The same benefit comes to those who invest energy in service-learning. At many colleges, students can discover what a teachable experience a few hours of service can be. As children we're taught that it's rude to expect something in return for something we've given. Could it be that service-learning is the delightful exception? It seems so, since we take up our role as a servant fully expecting to learn something from those we serve.

None of these venues is an escape from the real world; they are all doorways into it. When we pass through, we hear the world's celebrations and laments. If we listen with empathy, we discover what it means to hope the world's hopes — or maybe hope against them — for the sake of the kingdom of God.

According to Scripture, the person who wants the restoration of the earth wants the kingdom of God whether she knows it or not. And the coming of the kingdom depends on the coming of the King, the one who will return "with power and great glory" (Luke 21:27). However we are to understand this great, supernatural event, whatever form it takes, the second coming of Jesus Christ means to a

Christian that God's righteousness will at last fill the earth, and that the real world in all its trouble and turmoil will be transformed by God's shalom.

People with crummy lives want it to happen now. Passionate Christians *want* the return of the Lord. And, let me add, so do compassionate ones. When our own life is sweet, we can look across the world to lives that aren't sweet. We can raise our heads and our hopes for those lives. We can weep with those who weep and hope with those who hope. We can look across the world, and across the room, and across the hall. Could justice really come to the earth? Could husbands quit beating up their wives, and could wives quit blaming themselves? Could Palestinians and Israelis finally join hands? Could some of us who struggle with addictions or with diseases that trap us be liberated by God and start to walk tall in the kingdom of God? When God descends to us at the end, could we perhaps awaken *every* day to "stabs of joy" in mornings "too full of beauty" for us?

If we believe in the kingdom of God we will pray, and we will hope for those without much hope left. We will drive through the fog of doubt that descends on even the keenest believers. (So sturdy a Puritan as Increase Mather wrote in his diary for July 29, 1664, that he was "grieved, grieved, grieved with temptations to Atheisme.")[3] And one more tough thing. We will work and study in the same direction as we hope. According to Lewis Smedes, hoping for others is hard, but not the hardest. Praying for others is hard, but not the hardest. The hardest task for people who believe in the second coming of Jesus Christ is in "living the sort of life that makes people say, 'Ah, so *that's* how people are going to live when righteousness takes over our world.'"[4]

The hardest task is simple, persistent faithfulness in our work and in our attitudes — the kind of faithfulness that shows we are being drawn forward by the magnet force of the kingdom of God. Where learning is concerned, faithfulness means keeping at it long af-

3. Michael G. Hall, *The Last American Puritan: The Life of Increase Mather, 1629-1723* (Middletown, CT: Wesleyan University Press, 1988), 65.

4. Smedes, *Standing on the Promises*, 173.

ter a terminal degree. This means that even if you aren't thinking of pursuing graduate studies, your education ought never to end. Learning is a lifelong endeavor. That's why in one way it's not bad to think of your few years at college as a process of "learning how to learn." As we've already seen, learning isn't just for self-fulfillment or career enhancement. We learn in order to throw ourselves into the battle for the kingdom of God.

And it *is* a battle. The kingdom of God is in ceaseless conflict with the kingdoms of this world. The kingdoms of the world, the flesh, and the devil oppose the kingdom of God with all the powers they can muster. Education for the sake of the kingdom isn't a wholly safe undertaking. A Christian who goes to work for the kingdom simultaneously goes to war. What's needed on God's side are well-educated warriors. We are now fallen creatures in a fallen world. The Christian gospel tells us that all hell has broken loose in this sad world and that, in Christ, all heaven has come to do battle. Christ has come to defeat the powers and principalities, to move the world over onto a new foundation, and to equip a people — informed, devout, determined people — to lead the way in righting what's wrong, in transforming what's corrupted, in doing the things that make for peace, expecting that these things will travel across the border from this world to the new heaven and earth.

That's what Christian higher education is for. That's what all Christian education is for. Seen at its broadest reach, Christian education is for the kingdom of God. Christian higher education equips us to be agents of the kingdom, models of the kingdom in our own lives and communities, witnesses to the kingdom wherever we go in the world. In a fallen world, Christian education is a powerful engine for ministering to the world along the same line that we hope for the world.

From time to time we do need to see this big picture of the kingdom of God in order to find our calling inside its frame. But day to day, the issues of good and evil will come to us undramatically. They will come to us in a score of small questions that test and reveal our commitment to God's will on earth. How do I spend my time? How

143

do I spend my money? Why do so few of my good works really cost me something? How readily do I own up to messing up? How often do I think of Jesus Christ? How hard will I try to learn to spell and pronounce the name of an international student two doors down? When I daydream before falling asleep, whose happiness do I dream of?

Faithfulness in the small things can lead to faithfulness in the big things. What matters day by day is simple faithfulness to our calling, letting God decide the timetable for the great events, including the end of the human drama.

According to a story told by Os Guinness, an astute Christian social critic, the Connecticut House of Representatives was in session on a bright day in May, 1780, and the delegates were able to do their work by natural light. But then something happened that nobody expected. Right in the middle of debate, there was an eclipse of the sun and everything turned to darkness. Some of the legislators thought it was the Second Coming. So a clamor arose. People wanted to adjourn. People wanted to pray. People wanted to prepare for the coming of the Lord.

But the speaker of the House had a different idea and rose to the occasion with sound logic and good faith. We are all upset by the darkness, he said, and some of us are afraid. But, "the Day of the Lord is either approaching or it is not. If it is not, there is no cause for adjournment. And if the Lord *is* returning, I, for one, choose to be found doing my duty. I therefore ask that candles be brought."

And delegates who expected Jesus went back to their desks and resumed their debate.

Talking Points for Chapters 1 through 5

Chapter 1: Longing and Hope

- Agree or disagree: A person who didn't long for anything or anybody might be perfectly normal.
- What concrete steps might we take to expand our hopes for others?
- Why are peace and justice so often at the center of human hope?

Chapter 2: Creation

- If creation is in principle intelligible, does it follow that we ought to be able to explain it all? Scientists often study a particular life system with an eye on its possible contribution to *survival*. Would the discovery of survival value bring a Christian's search for intelligibility to its conclusion? Is survival value all that's interesting or significant about the way a created thing is put together?
- Paul says that corrupted human beings worship and serve "the creature rather than the Creator" (Rom. 1:25). Why is this a temptation?
- Genesis 1:27 has given some major theologians, including Karl Barth (undoubtedly the greatest Protestant theologian of the last century), the idea that maleness and femaleness together constitute an image of God. Why might this idea be at least plausible?

145

- How is mockery a kind of treason? Why have scorn and mockery become a significant part of popular entertainment, and why do people find them entertaining? Why, at the same time, are people in real life hypersensitive to the possibility that somebody has disrespected them?
- Most Christians think that the normal state of human beings is that of "embodied souls" or "besouled bodies" ("normal," because 2 Corinthians 5:1-8 and Philippians 1:23-24 suggest that we can exist in union with Christ without our bodies, albeit in a sort of plucked and chilly condition). In any case, let's suppose that our bodies are a truly important part, but not the whole, of who we are. What follows with respect to how seriously we ought to take our bodies? Should a person with a low-quality body take it that she has a low-quality life? Should a person with a high-quality body take it that he has a high-quality life? What are the lines of really *healthy* thinking about our relation to our bodies?

Chapter 3: The Fall

- As we've seen, bad characters make for a bad culture, but a bad culture also makes for bad characters. Think of star athletes who curse each other and spit on referees. Are these athletes leaders or followers? Are they corrupting the appetites of their youthful fans, or are they simply giving a debased culture what it already wants?
- Richard Rorty, one of America's most famous contemporary philosophers, states that he couldn't become a Christian because he couldn't manage to confess his sins in prayer to God. He simply couldn't get himself to do that.[1] Why is confession of sin so difficult? What sin *makes* confession of sin so difficult?
- Why does evil often look good to us, even exciting? Why do we find the story of a bank robbery more interesting than the story of a bank deposit?

1. Rorty, "There's No Big Picture," *University of Chicago Magazine*, April 1994, 20.

• Suppose a roommate drives drunk and endangers himself and others. Suppose we know this is wrong and foolish. Should we confront him? Would that be judgmental? Would it be *thought* to be judgmental? If so, would that settle the question? Would it be more important to preserve our own reputation for tolerance than to preserve the safety of people we care about? Ephesians 4:15 suggests that "speaking the truth in love" is a mark of a spiritual grown-up, and Galatians 6:1 counsels us to correct each other "in a spirit of gentleness." Both verses suggest that rebuking each other is delicate surgery that needs to be done carefully. Where will we learn it? Suppose there is a time to speak and a time for silence (Eccles. 3:7). How do we know which is which?

Chapter 4: Redemption

• Genesis 3 narrates the fall by picturing human shame and divine grace. Since then, have human beings needed salvation from unhealthy forms of shame as well as from guilt? Are there healthy forms of shame? One popular form of North American entertainment consists of explicit revelations of people's affairs, divorces, sex-change surgeries, body-part augmentations, etc. Assuming something is objectionable about these instances of spilling the beans, what is it? Are the revelations shameful? Shameless? Merely tacky? What kind of redemption is needed by a person who reveals too much?

• In recent years, North American courts and school districts have quarreled over the question whether public schools may post the Ten Commandments. Despite understandable concerns by the courts that public schools ought not to favor a particular form of religion, schools have persisted in wanting to post the Commandments. Why so? What civic good might be achieved by posting the Commandments? On the other hand, what significant part of their original context might get lost when the Commandments are displayed in secular settings?

147

- According to the Protestant reformers, salvation is by grace alone, through faith alone, in Christ alone. But if so, couldn't a person decide to coast? Couldn't a person decide to live however she wanted, thinking "I'm saved no matter what I do"? Alternatively, if we say that every regenerated person will certainly do good works and live a holy life — that, in fact, we can *tell* our faith by its fruits — won't we start anxiously introspecting? Won't we be tempted to fall back into the performance anxiety that God's grace is supposed to relieve?

- Given our differences in personal nature, and given our gender, racial, ethnic, and cultural differences, can the same rhythm of dying and rising sanctify us all? (Calvin called this rhythm "mortification and vivification.") Every day in India, a number of women are killed by husbands or fiancés because the woman's family didn't come up with a large enough dowry to please the killer. Even when permitted to live, women in many parts of the world are oppressed by daily humiliations intended to keep them in their place. If such women are, or become, Christians, must they still undergo the "mortification of their old nature"? Haven't they been mortified enough? Should a Christian missionary preach humility to people who have been humiliated for most of their lives?

  Calvin says that outside Christ we are trapped in a ceaseless oscillation between pride and despair. Do oppressors have more of the pride and victims more of the despair, so that when people die and rise with Christ they might start at different places? Should preachers and missionaries take this possibility into account, urging oppressors to repent and victims to hope in God? Or should preachers and missionaries preach exactly the same gospel, no matter who their audience is?

- In Romans 6 Paul writes that if you have died and risen with Christ you should "*consider* yourself dead to sin and alive to God." Apparently a believer needs faith not only in Jesus Christ, but also in her own sanctification. Why might this faith be necessary? Why might believers sometimes need to give themselves the benefit of the doubt where their own spiritual condition is concerned?

Chapter 5: Vocation in the Kingdom of God

- If everything God has made is potentially redeemable (see Chapter 2), does the same go for everything human beings have made? Are there cultural products so corrupt that Christians have to forget about trying to redeem them and have to try instead to abolish them? On what basis? May Christians try to do this politically even if others complain that we are then "imposing our values" on them? Is that always wrong to do? If it's sometimes wrong, what makes it wrong? Don't all laws impose on somebody's values?

- Suppose that all worthy occupations may become part of our vocation. Are all occupations worthy? Are there some legal occupations that serious Christians could not accept because there isn't much chance of contributing to the kingdom in these occupations? Could a serious Christian be a casino dealer, for example? A pro boxing promoter? A manufacturer of a flammable combat jelly that sticks to human skin and can't be extinguished? A designer of video games that reward ruthlessness? A truly swanky fashion show coordinator? A manufacturer of dolls designed to look just like the children who love them, so that when children look at what they love they're looking at themselves?

- English Puritans and many other Christians have developed a style of Christian faith that deliberately goes out to engage the world. "All of life is religious," they say. "Every square inch belongs to Jesus Christ." "There is no division between sacred and secular." Doesn't all this sound pretty worldly? What's to keep a world-engaging Christian from slipping into mere social activism? If "reforming the cities" is just as Christian as going to church, why bother going to church?

- How may Christians believe in both "the antithesis" (the enduring battle between good and evil) and common grace? Don't we have to choose?

- A Christian who observes contemporary culture — contemporary entertainment culture, for example — will observe a bewildering mix of good and evil.[2] She will find some healthy humor, but also some vile comedy. She will find a small amount of reverence, a small amount of overt blasphemy, and vast amounts of sheer, breezy indifference toward God. She will hear music that sounds like rebellion against creation and music that sounds like celebration of it. She will find scorn, cynicism, and an assumption to the effect that the pursuit of moral goodness is a quaint hobby of a few — perhaps something like stagecoach repair. She will find lots of gastrointestinal humor designed to make twelve-year-olds roar. She will also find, here and there and in unexpected places such as Hollywood, a film of such redemptive power (e.g., *Tender Mercies*) that it makes her weep.

Paul says, "hate what is evil, hold fast to what is good" (Rom. 12:9). But, as John Milton knew, "it was from out the rind of one apple tasted, that the knowledge of good and evil, as two twins cleaving together, leaped forth into the world."[3] How do you tell these twins apart? How do you *learn* to tell good from evil?

Milton says he doesn't trust a person's knowledge of goodness if that person hasn't gone out into the world to *test* his knowledge. A "cloistered virtue" doesn't help us. The point is that if we stay away from secular culture to protect ourselves from its temptations, we cannot live and witness in the real world. We can't even understand it.

But isn't there another side to this coin? Suppose we get close enough to secular culture to understand it, to witness to it, to try in some ways to reform it. How do we keep from being seduced by it?

2. As Frederick Buechner's character Godric says, "Nothing human's not a broth of false and true."

3. Milton, "Areopagitica," in *Complete Poems and Major Prose*, ed. Merritt Y. Hughes (New York: Odyssey, 1957), 728.